Summar

Biography

Readtrepreneur Publishing: Includes Summary of Killing Reagan & Summary of Killing the Rising Sun

By: Bill O' Reilyl & Martin Dugard

Proudly Brought to you by:

Text Copyright © Readtrepreneur

Legal & Disclaimer

The information contained in this book is not designed to replace or take the place of any form of medicine or professional medical advice. The information in this book has been provided for educational and entertainment purposes only.

The information contained in this book has been compiled from sources deemed reliable, and it is accurate to the best of the Author's knowledge; however, the Author cannot guarantee its accuracy and validity and cannot be held liable for any errors or omissions. Changes are periodically made to this book. You must consult your doctor or get professional medical advice before using any of the suggested remedies, techniques, or information in this book. Images used in this book is not the same as of that of the actual book. This is a totally separate and different entity from that of the original book titled: "Killing Reagan"

Upon using the information contained in this book, you agree to hold harmless the Author from and against any damages, costs, and expenses, including any legal fees potentially resulting from the application of any of the information provided by this guide. This disclaimer applies to any damages or injury caused by the use and application, whether directly or indirectly, of any advice or information presented, whether for breach of contract, tort, negligence, personal injury, criminal intent, or under any other cause of action.

You agree to accept all risks of using the information presented in this book. You need to consult a professional medical practitioner to ensure you are both able and healthy enough to participate in this program.

Table of Contents

The Book at a Glance

Killing Reagan: The Violent Assault That Changed a Presidency is the fifth nonfiction book by Fox News host Bill O'Reilly and collaborator Martin Dugard focusing on the "killing" of prominent historical personalities. He has followed this up with two other "Killing" books: *Killing the Rising Sun: How*

America Vanquished World War II Japan, and Killing England.

There is a significant difference between Killing Reagan and the four previous "killing" novels. In *Killing Reagan,* the protagonist, Reagan, is not assassinated, murdered or executed, as was the other historical figures in the four previous "killing" novels. In *Killing JFK,* for example, the book examines the shooting death of John F. Kennedy, by the assassin, Lee Harvey Oswald, as with the killing and Abraham Lincoln by John Wilkes Booth in *Killing Lincoln.* In an apparent Jewish-led conspiracy, Jesus Christ is crucified in *Killing Jesus,* and a dark and sinister plot by enemies of the U.S. in World War II succeeded in taking out General George S. Patton in *Killing Patton.*

Unlike the other Killing novels, Killing Reagan is a complete biographical sketch of Ronald Reagan's adult years spanning over fifty years, from his days as a radio reporter for baseball's Chicago Cubs, to his last days as an Alzheimer's-afflicted ex-president in his 90's. The authors weave in the otherwise unremarkable life of the would-be Reagan assassin, John Hinckley, Jr. into the tale of Reagan's extraordinary rise in American politics, towards their climactic crossing of paths in Hinckley, Jr.'s assassination attempt on March 30, 1981.

The book begins at the end of Ronald Wilson's long and

illustrious life. He is on his deathbed in his California ranch in Santa Barbara. The authors describe the shell of a man who was for most of his life, full of exuberance and vivaciousness. Watching him slip into the death is his biggest supporter, his wife of 42 years, Nancy and his children, some of which had significant disagreements with their parents, and led to a frosty relationship most of their lives, which was considerably warmed on this, the last day of their father.

Aside from his tentative first steps with celebrity in Hollywood, the book touches on his successes and failures as an entertainer, including a melancholy account of his days as a slapstick entertainer in Las Vegas, as he had fallen out of favor with Hollywood. The book briefly touches upon his romantic dalliances and failed marriage, and what would be a lifetime partnership with Nancy who would be by his side for almost fifty years as a wife, partner, and adviser.

A majority of the book, however, discusses the meteoric, but unexpected rise of Reagan in the world of politics, not just as a governor and president, but as an influence on the conservative movement in the United States even while he was sitting it out on the political sidelines. His face-off with Russian President Mikhail Gorbachev in the critical years of the Cold War would prove his mettle as a tough negotiator and diplomat.

The dark sidebar on this narrative is the sad and pitiable life of John Hinckley, Jr., the would-be Reagan assassin, whose mental imbalance would be a significant footnote in the Reagan anthology and popular culture, as he is somewhat associated with the actress Jodie Foster.

Then, there is the eventual decline and demise of one of the greatest leaders of not only the United States but the free world. From the moment that he is thrown off the horse to his last moments in the Santa Barbara ranch, the authors transport us to the grim denouement of the life of Ronald Wilson Reagan.

About the authors:

Bill O'Reilly, a lifelong journalist, has written or co-written over two dozen fiction and non-fiction books covering a wider variety of topics. He hosted a top-rated show, *The O'Reilly Factor* for many years at the Fox News Network before the network announced in April 2017 that they would not renew his contract as he battled a series of sexual harassment allegations.

Martin Dugard is a California-based writer who has written over a dozen books, including the seven *Killing* books with O'Reilly.

Prologue

June 5, 2004 - Ronald Reagan lapsed into a coma two days ago. His wife, Nancy, sits at the side of the bed, holding the former president's hand. Emotionally and physically exhausted by the ordeal, she quietly sobs as her body rocks in grief. Reagan's breathing has become ragged and inconsistent. After ten long years of slow descent toward the grave due to Alzheimer's disease, a bout of pneumonia brought on by food particles caught in his lungs has delivered the knockout blow.

Nancy knows that her beloved Ronnie's time has come. Ron, forty-six, and Patti, fifty-one, have been holding vigil with their mother for days. They have a reputation for conflict with their parents, but on this day, those quarrels have vanished as they lend their mother emotional support. An adopted son from Reagan's first marriage, Michael is not part of the final scene, as Ronald Reagan, once the leader of the free world, takes his last breath.

FREE BONUSES

P.S. Is it okay if we overdeliver?

Here at Readtrepreneur Publishing, we believe in overdelivering way beyond our reader's expectations. Is it okay if we overdeliver?

Here's the deal, we're going to give you an extremely condensed PDF summary of the book which you've just read and much more...

What's the catch? We need to trust you... You see, we want to overdeliver and in order for us to do that, we've to trust our reader to keep this bonus a secret to themselves? Why? Because we don't want people to be getting our exclusive PDF summaries even without buying our books itself. Unethical, right?

Ok. Are you ready?

Firstly, remember that your book is code: "**READ47**".

Next, visit this link: **http://bit.ly/exclusivepdfs**

Everything else will be self explanatory after you've visited: **http://bit.ly/exclusivepdfs.**

We hope you'll enjoy our free bonuses as much as we enjoyed preparing it for you!

Chapter 1

The narrative jumps to Reagan's 1980 presidential debate with sitting Democratic president Jimmy Carter, who is content in his belief that Ronald Reagan is nowhere his intellectual equal, aside from calling Reagan, "untruthful and dangerous," and telling the debate audience that the choice between him and Reagan is, "a choice between two futures."

In a way, Carter, an Annapolis-trained scholar, is right about the not-so-great intellect of Reagan, who struggled to keep a C average in a small Illinois college. But Reagan is a deep thinker with big ideas, and more critical in these staged debates, he can memorize scripts reasonably quickly, letting his actor training kick in. The Reagan team has also "cheated" for this event, allowing Reagan to know in advance how Carter will respond to every debate question. But Reagan's debate weaponry includes the lines, "There you go again," when Carter spouts his tired references to his daughter Amy's comments and asking the audience, "Are you better off than you were four years ago?," which the United States was probably not. Even if it was, the voting population certainly felt things were worse.

The answer is so apparent, and the election turns out to be a landslide for Ronald Reagan who receives 489 electoral votes; to Jimmy Carter's 49.

The busy chapter includes an introduction to John Hinckley Jr. and his fixation on then child actress Jodie Foster, who is starred opposite Robert De Niro in the 1976 movie Taxi Driver—a film Hinckley had seen multiple times.

Chapter 2

It is 1937, and Ronald Reagan is a twenty-six-year-old sports reporter for a Des Moines, Iowa radio station covering the Chicago Cubs. As he steps down from the electric trolley at the Republic Pictures stop in Hollywood, he admits later to friend Joy Hodge, a friend from Des Moines that he was starry-eyed, and overwhelmed by the power of Hollywood.

Joy Hodge believes that Reagan possesses the confident good looks that give him a chance to make it in Hollywood. She sets up a meeting between her agent and Reagan, who gives him a screen test. He is at least attractive enough for Warner Bros. head Jack Warner to offer him a seven-year contract that will pay him three times as much as his sports reporter salary: two hundred dollars a week,

Reagan meets a Sarah Jane Mayfield a.k.a. Jane Wyman, a beautiful actress who at the time was married to a millionaire businessman. She falls in love with Reagan and quickly gets a divorce. They are dubbed as Hollywood's golden couple in a highly public romance, where and renowned (and feared) gossip columnist Louella Parsons calls them "wholesome and happy and utterly completely American."

Reagan is commissioned as a second lieutenant in the U.S. Army in 1942, making training films and selling war bonds. He returns from the war, and he gets an even more lucrative contract from Warner Brothers: a multi-year deal that would guarantee him at least $52,000 per picture. Reagan and Wyman move into a five-thousand-square-foot custom showcase home in Los Angeles, and their Hollywood royalty reputation grows.

Their marriage is shattered when their first baby is born prematurely and survives only nine hours, and Reagan is not even at her side when Wyman gives birth. But they eventually have a daughter, Maureen, in the midst of their rising careers. As the couple gets busier with their acting careers, Wyman is losing her affection for Reagan who she feels is increasingly condescending towards her. She feels out of his depth when Reagan talks about his political activism. Things come to a head when she tells him "Shut up and go shit in your hat," after a lengthy speech in front of the Screen Actors Guild.

They divorced soon after and Reagan falls into a deep depression that he masks by drinking and womanizing. He becomes a serial womanizer, and proposes marriage to a much younger actress, Christine Larson, who turns him down, further worsening his depression. His career takes a dive, the nadir being his playing second fiddle to a chimpanzee in the film, *Bedtime for Bonzo.*

As his acting career takes a dive, his political awareness begins to soar. He develops a distaste for communism as he begins to take on an activist role in politics.

Chapter 3

In the midst of his womanizing, Reagan meets Nancy Davis, an actress ten years his junior. Reagan is unsure about the relationship because he is still seeing other women. With his acting career on the decline, he formalizes his entrée into the political world by joining Crusade for Freedom, an anti-communist group. It is secretly bankrolled by the Central Intelligence Agency to fight communist propaganda all over the world.

But even as his roles and acting career are diminished, he is still popular enough within his own circles to be elected president of the Screen Actors' Guild. His involvement in Hollywood continues.

On September 27, 1946, Reagan got his first hands-on experience with communist activism when union leader Herb Sorrell leads a violent protest against the Warner Brothers studio. His anti-communist initiative intersects with his acting career as he testifies in front of the House Un-American Activities Committee, a congressional group led by Senator Joseph McCarthy. Reagan names six actors suspected of being communists, who are banned for 20 years each from acting in Hollywood.

Chapter 4

In 1951, Reagan made a simple, and to Nancy's mind, unromantic proposal, "Let's get married," over dinner at a Los Angeles nightclub shortly after Davis told him she was pregnant.

A year later, in 1952, Ronald Reagan puts his womanizing ways behind him and marries Nancy Davis. With her new husband, Nancy sees greatness in Reagan that she feels has so far eluded him. She possesses an inner strength and hardness that her husband seems to lack, and she is intent to make it a mission in life to bring this greatness forward. But all the happiness is muted when he learns that he has just been released from his contract with Warner Brothers.

Chapter 5

Reagan's entertainment career plummets to new lows two years later, 1954, as he ends up doing a cheesy late night act in the Last Frontier Hotel and Casino, in Las Vegas. Throughout the show, Nancy Reagan, a non-smoker, is sitting alone, nursing some water, and is enveloped by a thick cloud of cigarette smoke.

Nancy sees all of this as a humiliating nadir in her husband's entertainment career. She watches Ronald Reagan deliver tasteless underwear jokes in twice-nightly performances six days a week, with a 1:30 matinee thrown in on Saturdays, and she endures each and every show. It is the best paying gig that Reagan can get, a gig that he needs to support his wife and new child, Patti, as well as two children from his previous marriage to Wyman. They also have two mortgages to worry about, together with some back taxes.

Things turn around quickly, however. He is offered $125,000 per year to host a Sunday night show titled, General Electric Theater, which will be more than enough to take care of their financial obligations, including their mortgages. The show is a big hit, and his finances quickly recover, and his reputation grows as a topnotch PR guy.

But there is more than just being an emcee for General Electric, a giant corporation with numerous factories and thousands of workers.   He sees how government interference effects, sometimes for the worse, commercial activity.   His political urges are rekindled after the embarrassing interregnum in Las Vegas. On his travels throughout the country, he writes careful speeches on stacks of 3 x 5 index cards – one day to be combined into one spectacular thesis that will be famously known as "The Speech."

Chapter 6

It is early in the morning on May 29, 1955, and John Hinckley, Sr., a successful oilman, is awaiting the delivery of his child. A deeply religious man, he is in the maternity ward of the soon-to-close two-story, brick building that is the Hardy Sanitarium Hospital. His wife, 28-year-old JoAnn has chosen to deliver in this hospital instead of the spanking new state-of-the-art Memorial Hospital. While Hinckley, Sr. had once envisioned that his expected-for son would be the first boy born at Memorial, it would turn out that his new child would be the last boy born in Hardy. Hinckley, Sr. promised that he would name his son, John, Jr. if things went his way.

At 6 a.m., the senior Hinckley gets his wish. John Warnock Hinckley Jr. is born in an old mental hospital, instead of a spanking new state-of-art medical facility. One day, because of his son, John, Sr. will be fending off whispers that he has ties with the Central Intelligence Agency, whispers that will be taken seriously by the U.S. government and the media. It will also be ironic that less than thirty years later, John, Jr. will end up in a mental hospital as an adult.

Chapter 7

Five years later, in 1960, John F. Kennedy is accepting the nomination as the Democratic candidate for president. Ronald Reagan watches and is disgusted by the speech, which he believes is a concession to government interference and communism, Reagan decides that as a registered Democrat, will vote for Kennedy's opponent, outgoing Republican Vice-President Richard Nixon.

After World War II, the movie industry was deeply divided between conservatives, such as Reagan and John Wayne, and more significant number of liberals, led by singer Frank Sinatra and his Rat Pack, who had fallen under John F. Kennedy's spell. Sinatra, one of the brightest stars, despises both Ronald and Nancy Reagan.

Reagan immediately writes Nixon, to warn him about the growing role of the federal government and increased government spending, if Kennedy is elected president. Reagan, who believes that Kennedy is Karl Marx in disguise, is regarded very lightly by Nixon, who considers Reagan, an intellectual lightweight. Kennedy narrowly defeats Nixon to become president, and two years later, Reagan switches his party affiliation to Republican.

Four years later, on October 27, 1964, Ronald Reagan watches a speech that he taped a week before in support of Republican presidential nominee, Arizona Senator Barry Goldwater. With nary a mention of the nominee, Reagan launches into a twenty-seven-minute oration that extols the virtues of America. It is a dazzling speech filled with references to the American dream, fiscal conservatism, and small government. The statement will come to be known as, "A Time for Choosing," and will be such a big hit that it generates a massive deluge of support and money for Goldwater, who loses the election despite the Reagan assist. Reagan's speech is considered one of the most significant American political statements.

Chapter 8

In January 1967, Ronald Reagan was inaugurated as California's governor. Becoming chief executive of the U.S.'s largest state has transformed him from a girl-chasing Lothario to a reinvented father image to his constituents. His election also means two things: his and Nancy's reliance on astrology will deepen, and the massive pay cut he will take to become Governor of California means that they will need to sell their Malibu ranch.

Reagan agrees to a debate with prospective Democratic presidential nominee Robert Kennedy in the show, *Town Meeting of the World*, where Kennedy defends students demonstrating the Vietnam War, absolving them of any impact on the lengthening of the war. When Reagan's turn to speak comes up, he confidently asserts that the student demonstrations are prolonging the war, and excoriates them. Kennedy then apologizes on behalf of the country for mistakes in American foreign policy leading to the Vietnam War.

Reagan effortlessly reels off facts about the War, and attacks the U.S.'s enemies instead of blaming America for the conflict. Reagan turns the discussion from Vietnam and begins to talk about the greatness of the United States. He has crushed Robert Kennedy by being bolder and confident about America's importance and potential. Many see the debate as things to come between two protagonists in future presidential elections. This does not come to pass, however, as Kennedy is assassinated barely a year later near the lobby of a Los Angeles hotel.

While Kennedy's presidential aspirations are snuffed with an assassin's bullet, Reagan is optimistic about his plans to run for president in 1968. These plans are scuttled, however, when a scandal regarding the homosexual affair of two of his staffers blows up. The Republican nominee is Richard Nixon, who will defeat Democrat Hubert Humphrey, to become the 37th president of the United States.

Chapter 9

Six years later, the Watergate scandal forces Richard Nixon to resign the presidency. While Nixon is about to leave the nation's highest office in shame, Ronald Reagan has achieved a lot in his two terms as California governor. He cracked down on violent student protests in Vietnam, balanced the budget, and even became Nixon's special envoy to China, traveling there four times. He also managed to make a friend of former detractor Frank Sinatra, Jr.

On the night that Nixon has announced his intention to resign as president; Reagan gives Nixon a "courtesy call," even as both men secretly dislike each other. They are in a battle for control of the Republican Party, and Nixon, at the twilight of his political career, feels threatened by Reagan's popularity. He is torn about who to name as his successor and was first inclined to nominate John Connally for vice president. Connally was a lifelong Democrat who had just switched party affiliation which meant that his nomination may face some serious problems. Nixon's second choice is Nelson Rockefeller, and his third, Ronald Reagan, who is extremely popular among Republicans. But because of envy on Nixon's part, he chooses Michigan Congressman Gerald

Ford, the House minority leader, instead.

After Nixon resigns, Ronald Reagan wonders if Gerald Ford will select him to be the vice president of the United States, but Ford chooses Spiro Agnew instead.

Chapter 10

It is 1974, and nineteen-year-old John Hinckley Jr. lies around in his tidy Dallas, Texas rented an apartment, strumming on his guitar. The spartan room is neat, as Hinckley is a fanatic about cleanliness and personal hygiene, often washing his face with such vigor that his father fears "he'd take the skin off."

Born into a family of achievers, Hinckley finds himself working part-time in a pizza joint, sweeping floors and cleaning bathrooms during the summer school break. Hinckley is a loner who hardly smiles, and has no interest in keeping fit, and especially no interest in presidential politics. He is afflicted with a form of schizophrenia, which gives him a sense of distorted reality. He is slowly withdrawing from society and appears incapable of experiencing happiness. They do not recognize this withdrawal until it is too late.

Chapter 11

It is 1975, and the comedian Chevy Chase is making a career out of making fun of Gerald Ford, whose presidency is being notoriously remembered for the pardon of Richard Nixon, and the fall of Vietnam to communist forces. He appears to be ripe for defeat in the 1976 nomination for the Republicans.

Ronald Reagan, the would-be challenger, has already been spurned by both Richard Nixon and Ford and is now an ex-governor whose primary occupation is to travel the world giving speeches, but making tons of money in the process. Also, he has two ghostwriters who help him with a weekly syndicated newspaper column which is printed in 226 papers across the United States. In one of his activities after he steps down as California governor, he pays a courtesy visit to Margaret Thatcher, who is making waves as the new House of Commons opposition leader in the United Kingdom. The 49-year old Thatcher is one of the new breeds of British politicians, who are fighting to wean her nation out of the cradle-to-grave welfare attitude that has saddled the British economy since the end of World War II.

Thatcher on the surface seems to be a homely woman, but Reagan sees the steely resolve in her. She also shares his passionate disdain for communism, and their friendship will evolve to a very close one, culminating in them calling each other, "ideological soul mates." They meet for two hours, and Reagan judges her to be "warm, feminine, gracious, and intelligent." Their friendship is cemented amidst the gloom of the United States withdrawing from the war, efficiently accepting defeat in the hands of communists.

On the domestic front, Nancy is having her own troubles. Oldest daughter Patti has moved in with a rock musician and is openly smoking marijuana. Meanwhile, 17-year old son Ron was discovered seducing the 30-year wife of musician Ricky Nelson right in her own bedroom. Nancy's other personal challenge is that she is beginning to resent the growing celebrity status of Betty Ford, the First Lady, who is much more appreciated by the American public than her husband. The feeling of disdain is mutual, as Mrs. Ford considers Nancy, a "cold fish."

Their enmity comes to a head when the Fords invite the Reagans to dinner, with the express purpose of convincing Reagan not to challenge Ford for the Republican nomination in 1976. He knows that Reagan, who he considers an intellectual inferior, will be a formidable opponent because of his overwhelming support of the party's conservative base.

He offers Reagan a spot on his cabinet, and when Nelson Rockefeller decides to step down as Vice-President, that office is open to him as well. Reagan will not go for anything less than the presidential nomination, and he declines Ford's offers.

In the final tally of primary votes, Gerald Ford's barely beats Reagan, 1,187 votes to 1,070. Reagan graciously delivers his concession speech and draws five-minute applause from an admiring convention crowd.

Ronald Reagan waves goodbye to a stunned, but the charmed crowd. As he walks away, they realize that their party has just nominated the wrong candidate to be the President of the United States.

Chapter 12

It is the night before the 1976 elections, and Ronald Reagan refuses to commit publicly whether he will run for president again in four years. He variously tells people that he won't rule it out, but he also wouldn't "rule it in." Nancy Reagan, however, is acting as if the decision had already been made, as she and her husband appear to be courting severe supporters. Reagan spends the morning of Election Day in his office, composing handwritten letters to supporters. The couple is driven to Hollywood, where Nancy listens to her husband record twenty radio commentaries.

Nancy allows her husband to concentrate on his politics, while she has to do practically everything else, including having to deal with her increasingly complicated children. She grapples with the drama of her daughter Patti's increasingly tempestuous life, including her alleged involvement with illegal drugs as well as numerous changes of boyfriends. Nancy is also getting increasingly worried that Ron Reagan Jr. is another liberal who baldly flaunts his opposition to his parents' conservatism. He now studies ballet and makes it a point to wear his hair too long in public. It is also becoming very apparent that her husband's children with Jane Wyman,

Maureen, and Michael, don't like her, and are drifting further and further away. Still, it all seems worth it because she feels that her husband finally realizes his potential. Reagan has become a powerful man, and his income has increased significantly because of his radio contracts and speeches.

In the meantime, Gerald Ford is sweating out the election results, with most polls calling it a toss-up. In a matter of hours, he will know whether the country has fired him from his job. In the early morning after Election Day, they find out that they have lost the election to Jimmy Carter.

Nancy Reagan begins her planning for 1980, for the one job that her husband just needs to have.

Chapter 13

It is the summer of 1976, and Hinckley is now in Hollywood, California, alone in an aging movie theater watching the movie, *Taxi Driver*, for the 15th or so time. The 21-year old Hinckley is falling deeply in love with the movie's star, Jodie Foster, and doesn't care how old she is.

John Hinckley, Jr. has come to Hollywood to become a star and was counting on his guitar skills to become a star, in the process becoming rich and famous. His Hollywood dream, however, has not happened, and he finds himself languishing in a squalid apartment building off Sunset Boulevard that he pays by the week to live in. He becomes increasingly isolated and lonely, living on fast food, and beginning to entertain irrational thoughts, such as Blacks and Jews being the enemies of white men like him. He only contacts his parents when he needs money and continues to lie to them about his status, convincing them that he is doing better than he actually is, such as telling them about a non-existent rock music demo he supposedly recorded.

He will start acting like Travis Bickle, Robert de Niro's character in *Taxi Driver*. He keeps a journal like the Bickle character, and will soon possess the one thing that Travis Bickle has that he doesn't own: a gun.

Chapter 14

It is 1980, an election year, and President Jimmy Carter is depressed. Inflation and unemployment keep on increasing while his poll numbers continue to go south. To top it off, a daring rescue attempt to save American embassy hostages held in Iran is a catastrophic failure. A helicopter carrying the would-be rescuers of the hostage's crashes, and the rescue attempt is aborted. Eight American servicemen die, and America's enemies gloat about the failure. Instead of talking paternally to his nation to soothe Americans about the failure, he carries on like the naval officer that he is, unemotionally explaining his failed tactics to a grieving nation, hoping against hope that the empty words might just save his struggling re-election campaign.

His most likely primary opponent is yet another Kennedy, Edward, or Ted, who has his own "crash" scandal to deal with. Just over ten years earlier on July 18, 1969, the senator from Massachusetts was coming from a party on Chappaquiddick Island, a short ferry ride from Kennedy's hamlet on Martha's Vineyard, when he drives his car off a bridge into a canal. The crash kills a beautiful young campaign worker, 28-year old Mary Jo Kopechne, because of

Kennedy's delay in calling for help. The many innuendos, whether they were true or not, put a permanent stain on Kennedy's legacy, and it was left to be seen whether the incident would still haunt him in the 1980 presidential primaries. It soon becomes apparent that this incident has fatally injured this, and any future presidential campaign and Carter becomes the Democratic candidate again, almost by default.

Reagan, meanwhile, has locked up his party's nomination, accommodates his closest Republican rival and vehement critic, George H. W. Bush. He offers Bush the vice presidential slot at the Republican nominating convention in New York City.

Reagan's defeat of Carter was such a landslide that Jimmy Carter conceded the election to Reagan even before the polls closed in California. The Reagans' astrologer has it all wrong this time. She predicted that now President and Nancy Reagan would spend a long night awaiting the returns of the election.

Chapter 15

In October 1980, John Hinckley, Jr. was shuttling from state to state, and wandering to find his niche since his lost summer in Los Angeles. In the course of his meandering, he often returned to Texas Tech University in Lubbock, Texas, getting B's and C's in the few courses that he took. But the constant in his life is his deepening fascination with Jodie Foster. He continues to write her poems and letters and is even able to contact her by phone. She finds him rude, creepy, and dangerous and tells him never to contact her again. Devastated by Foster's spurning, Hinckley attempts to commit suicide by ingesting anti-depressants, but even in that venture, he fails. He then goes to another Travis Bickle tactic for romancing women – political assassination.

He has since become a fan of Adolf Hitler and even bought a two-volume set of the Hitler's ideological masterpiece, *Mein Kampf.* He takes neo-Nazi leader Michael Allen's exhortation to heart, that public demonstrations and rallies are not enough, and that violence and bloodshed are the correct answers.

Hinckley, who has followed Jimmy Carter in his campaign stops in Ohio, supports the President to Nashville. He plans to assassinate President Carter so that he can impress Jodie Foster; with the assassination plan coming straight out of the script of *Taxi Driver*.

Looking nervous in the airport with loaded guns in his suitcase, he tries to get through without having his suitcase scanned. However, Evelyn Braun and Laura Farmer of the Wackenhut Security Corporation are suspicious of Hinckley's demeanor. Braun instructs Farmer to pay closer attention to the X-ray of Hinckley's bag. The x-ray reveals that he indeed has weapons in his bag and is arrested. They arrest a terrified Hinckley and charge him with possession of firearms.

He is brought in front of Judge William E. Higgins, who swiftly delivers a guilty verdict. There will be no jail time, and Hinckley is ordered to surrender his weapons, pay a $50 fine, and $12.50 in court costs. He walks out the courtroom a free man. Relieved, he rushes to the airport, where he gets on the next plane to Dallas.

In 1980, the Secret Service developed a computer file listing four hundred men and women authorities feel are the most likely people to attempt a presidential assassination. They also come up with a second list of over 25,000 people who might be capable of such an act. Because of Carter's visit to Nashville, the FBI is overwhelmed and fails to conduct an in-depth interrogation of Hinckley. He does not show up on either list, despite his troubles in Nashville.

Chapter 16

It is January 1981, and the Reagans are attending their ninth inaugural ball of the evening, this one a gala organized by one-time critic Frank Sinatra. The emcee is Johnny Carson, and many Hollywood stars, like Bob Hope, are in attendance. The ticket to the main dinner, which was in such high demand, goes for $500 a plate, and the party is filled with formally dressed men and women noisily enjoying the trappings of wealth and power. It is a far cry from the muted "celebration" after Jimmy Carter's inauguration, where he did not feel it appropriate to host even a single ball, let alone ten. Carter's inaugural speech was expectedly somber, pointing out America's limitations, in stark opposition to Reagan's optimistic view of America.

In the midst of the glitz and celebration, many wonder about Ronald Reagan's health. He assumed the presidency at 69, taking on a job that is notorious for quickening the aging process. But despite his age, the worst of his ailments are a slight hay fever and minor arthritis in his right thumb. A shattered femur suffered in a celebrity baseball game years ago, is no longer a factor. Reagan works out every night before taking an evening shower, in a defiant display of his strength and health. The president, in the objective view of many health professionals, is in remarkable physical shape for his age.

There is also some buzz about his supposedly average intellect. But over the years, his deep curiosity about economic and political issues has allowed him to understand the nuances of foreign and domestic policy. He also has a remarkable ability to remember the minutest facts in his speeches and debates.

In the process of becoming a staunch anti-communist, Ronald Reagan discovered a new political hero. His former idol, Democrat Franklin Delano Roosevelt, has been replaced by former Republican president Calvin Coolidge, a quiet man who did not even run for a second term, despite his popularity. Reagan credits Coolidge as an unassuming man who got things done efficiently, and "in a quiet way." During the Reagan administration, Coolidge's picture will hang in the Cabinet Room of the White House.

Despite the religious right forming a sizeable percentage of his voting bloc, Ronald Reagan does not pander to voters by invoking religion. The Reagans rarely go to church, and when asked about the country's most divisive religious issue, abortion, he gives a terse reply about abortion being the equivalent of taking a human life, and not conforming to the Judeo-Christian values of the country.

He is despised by many in the media because an overwhelming majority simply does not agree with his politics. They dismiss him as a dangerous, lightweight; a former B-movie actor impersonating a politician. A very small circle of people know the real Ronald Reagan, including, sadly, his own children, for whom he has put minimal effort into fatherhood. He is an intensely private but loyal man and exposes very little of himself to other people. His world revolves around his conservative politics, and of course, Nancy, with whom Reagan has been known to be annoyed with, but rarely gets angry with. Most of the American public will just have to satisfy themselves with Reagan cutting the image of a benevolent father figure, a man who makes themselves proud to be American.

Nancy Reagan, on the other hand, is an open book, avoids minimal conflict, and will confront all critics and enemies of his husband and family. She is known to just blurt out what she feels, without fear of reprisal or consequences. She is intensely protective of her husband and her entire family, even when their children apparently do not approve of much of what she does or what she stands for. For example, she refuted gun control in a way that her husband wouldn't, by saying that she owns a tiny little gun herself. Critics call her cheap and self-absorbed, and Johnny Carson calls her the "Evita of Bel-Air," comparing Mrs. Reagan to the Argentinian dictator. It is a given that Nancy Reagan, for better or for worse, will be an integral part of Reagan's White House brain trust as long as he is president.

In his first White House term, Ronald Reagan selects an experienced political insider, James Baker III as his chief of staff. As deputy, he picks Michael Deaver, a loyal member of Reagan's California gubernatorial staff, who Ronald and Nancy Reagan prize for his loyalty. The third man is attorney Edwin Meese, Reagan's chief of staff while he was governor of California. He has often been called Reagan's alter-ego because he and Reagan know each other so well. Thanks to this capable team, and of course, Nancy, Reagan is confident that he can run the country efficiently.

Chapter 17

On March 7, 1981, John Hinckley, Jr. got off the United Airlines flight from New York courtesy of his parents. He is tired and unshaven, coming off another worthless trip to the East Coast, with the familiar result of getting spurned once again by Jodie Foster. He sent Foster a love letter while she was studying at Yale University, which Foster turned over to the Yale University campus police. The police immediately launch an investigation into Hinckley's whereabouts, as he writes his mom and once again asks for help.

Hinckley is one of the last passengers to get down from the plane. Awaiting him is his disappointed father, Jack, who left his mother behind at home in Evergreen because she has spent the entire day crying about John Hinckley, and his latest disappointing venture for self-improvement. In fact, every Hinckley family member is distraught by John's behavior.

His mother had asked her son to consult with a Colorado psychiatrist, Dr. John Hopper, regarding what his family perceives as a mental health issue. Dr. Hopper, however, does not see anything particularly alarming about John Hinckley's mental state after meeting with him. In their irregularly scheduled sessions, Dr. Hopper just believes that his parents, having coddled him for a long time, are responsible for his behavior. He tells John's parents that they need to put their foot down and hold their son accountable for his life and his future.

Based on Dr. Hopper's evaluation, Jack and Jo Ann Hinckley give their son an ultimatum: He needs to have gotten a job by March 1, 1987, or he must move out of their home within a month. March 7 comes and goes, and Hinckley still has not found a job. Dr. Hopper orders the couple to tell their son, "goodbye," give him a hundred dollars, and let him loose.

With his son not meeting their ultimatum, a heartbroken Jack Hinckley, in the middle of a busy Denver airport, must accomplish a gut-wrenching piece of parenting: he must kick his son out of their lives and tell him good-bye. He says, John, that the family has reached the end of the rope, unable to figure out what he had been doing.

The abrupt "dismissal" stuns John Hinckley; who at the age of twenty-five, is so used to having his problems solved by his parents. It is a singularly sad moment for both father and son, more so probably for Jack, who watches his son leave. They would not see each other again until several weeks later, in the visiting room of a prison.

John shows up again three weeks later, parking his car in front of his parents' driveway. He has been living at a roach motel, the Golden Palms Hotel, barely half an hour away from his parents' home.   John tells his mother that he is flying off to California, to start a new life, not knowing that stashed in his luggage is one of John's RG-14 .22-caliber Saturday Night Specials.

Chapter 18

It is March 3, 1981, and Walter Cronkite, a legend in television broadcasting; the man that America trusts when it comes to delivering the news, is seated in the Diplomatic Reception Room, making small talk with Ronald Reagan.

Cronkite, the CBS anchorman, later on, to be revealed as a liberal, wants to ask the president hard questions about whether he plans to wage nuclear war with the Soviet Union. In recent weeks, Reagan had talked tough about his stance on the Soviet Union, pointing out the same disdain and disgust for communism that he had when he was going against the Hollywood Communists almost forty years earlier.

Just over a week before his interview, on February 24, his Soviet counterpart, President Leonid Brezhnev delivered a three-hour discourse in Moscow in front of Communist Party leaders, emphasizing his commitment to Russia's defense. Over his almost seventeen years of running the country, Brezhnev has overseen the secret increase in the nuclear arsenal, expansion of its military that dwarfs the United States', and a general aggressive path versus the United States and the Western world, in general.

Cronkite, a closet anti-war crusader, tries to put Reagan on the defensive by talking about a "crisis" in the United States' foreign policy, likening the Reagan administration's dilemma with the problems related to military advisers in Central America. He makes special mention of El Salvador, likening the initial incursion of that country with the United States' entry into the Vietnam War. Cronkite's questioning seems to try to test Reagan's resolve and his command of the facts. Cronkite also seems to suggest, that the right approach seems to be conducting a meeting with the Russians and come up with some sort of accommodation to get past this "danger point."

But Reagan will not be derailed in his rhetoric against the Soviet Union. He says that it has been a while since an American president has openly challenged the Soviet Union. Displaying a command of the facts, he rattles off the details of the growing Russian, and Cuban-backed Communist presence in Central America. He is adamant that detente' will not work and is a phony concept. He tells Cronkite that it is foolish and suicidal for the United States to unilaterally disarm itself; losing all negotiating value when it sits down with Russia, who will have all the arms. Reagan, as he has all his life, despises communism and its leaders, and knows that he has one, and maybe, two presidential terms to reduce the Soviet threat.

Not used to public offensive rhetoric against himself and the Soviet Union, an angry Brezhnev furiously composes and dictates a nine-page response to Reagan, in the form of a personal letter. Brezhnev insists that while his country has no intention to ramp up the arms race, he says that he will not allow any country to establish superiority over the Soviet Union. He tells Reagan that continued escalation of the arms race is dangerous madness.

Reagan must craft a response to Brezhnev's letter, and he consults with his advisers. This time, he turns to Secretary of State Alexander Haig, to draft the letter. Reagan plans to review the letter as soon as it is done and send it to Brezhnev. But the letter will not be sent because John Hinckley, Jr. will soon make everyone change their plans.

Chapter 19

On the morning of March 30, 1981, John Hinckley is in Washington, D.C. making plans for what to him, should be a momentous day. He has alternative plans to make himself famous on this day. His first option is to go to New Haven, CT, and shoot himself in front of Jodie Foster at Yale University. His second option is to be the third assassin of a Kennedy brother, devising a plan to shoot Ted Kennedy. Third, he will go to the Capitol's U.S. Senate chamber and kill as many lawmakers as he can. Finally, his most significant and boldest plan – the assassination of the President of the United States.

At the same moment, two blocks away in the White House, President Ronald Reagan is just concluding a ceremonial fourteen-minute meeting in the Cabinet Room with a group of Hispanic leaders. He returns to his White House residence, changes into a blue suit, and sits down to review a speech he will be making to liberal union members at the Washington Hilton. He has a short lunch with a friend before preparing to leave for his speech.

As the president eats lunch, John Hinckley is showering in his motel room. While he is going over his choices as to who to kill, an article on page 4 of the Washington Star newspaper catches his attention. There is an article, "President's Schedule," which mentions that the President will be delivering a speech at the Washington Hilton that very afternoon. It is the most convenient play, and Hinckley decides that he will go to the Hilton. Before leaving, he writes a letter to Jodie Foster saying that, "There is a definite possibility I will be killed in my attempt to get Reagan." He leaves this letter in a suitcase so that investigators may see it after he carries out the assassination. At 12:45 p.m., he leaves for the Washington Hilton with his gun.

At 2:24, Reagan finishes his speech and begins to file out of the hotel's VIP entrance together with his secret service detail and his staff, including Press Secretary James Brady, and they head for the presidential limousine. Hinckley stands just outside the entrance with dozens of onlookers crowding each other to get a glimpse of the President.

At 2:27, Hinckley fires his first shot. It hits Brady squarely on the head, above his left eye, and falls on the ground, face first. His second bullet hits Washington Metro police officer Thomas K. Delahanty in the neck and the bullet lodges against his spinal column. The third shot goes wild, while the fourth bullet hits Secret Service agent Tim McCarthy in the torso, and gets lodged in his liver. The fifth and sixth bullets bounce off the limousine, but the last one ricochets off the car, and pierces Reagan just below his left arm, enters his lung, and lodges an inch from his heart. It takes Hinckley less than 2 seconds to fire all six bullets.

Reagan is pushed into the limousine by Secret Service agent Jarry Parr, and the limousine takes just 4 minutes to bring him to George Washington University Hospital. Nancy Reagan is at the White House and is informed of the assassination attempt, and she rushes to the hospital to be with her husband. She finds him pale and weak, and her knees shake, and she is unsteady, as she watches her husband get wheeled into the emergency operating room on a gurney.

In the meantime, the United States is still a country that needs to be run. The media, already aware of the assassination attempt, wonders who is running the country. They ask a bewildered Larry Speakes, the Deputy Press Secretary, who mutters, "I cannot answer that question at this time," because, at the very moment, nobody really knows. Vice President George H. W. Bush is in an airplane over Texas, on his way to Washington D.C.

The cabinet members huddled in the White House Situation Room, are dismayed with Speakes' distressing, yet truthful statement. The scary truth is that no one present in the White House has the authority to respond to emergencies like this and a Soviet attack, if and when it comes. Preparing for the worst-case scenario, Richard Allen, the National Security Adviser orders "the football," be brought to him. The football is the legendary briefcase that holds the launch codes for nuclear missiles that could give rise to World War III.

But suddenly, the Secretary of State, Gen. Alexander Haig, takes charge of the situation and installs himself as the country's temporary president. The presidential succession order places him as the fourth in the pecking order in case the President of the United States cannot fulfill his duties. In a sense, therefore, Haig is breaking the law.

But the chaos is finally defused, when at 6:46 p.m., an unconscious Ronald Reagan is sewn up, then brought from the operating room – a great crisis has passed. His return marks the end of Haig's three-hour, self-declared reign as United States President.

Chapter 20

On the morning of April 28, 1981, both Houses of Congress get on their feet to give a rousing standing ovation to the President who had just survived an assassination attempt barely five weeks earlier. The bipartisan cheers are for a survivor who looks visibly more frail and thinner but is moving comfortably on his own power. He approaches the podium amidst a mighty roar of welcome. He is squarely back in the saddle as he warmly shakes the hand of his Vice-President, who was on the brink of assuming the presidency, and Massachusetts Speaker of the House Tip O'Neill, a fellow Irishman, and a Democrat with which Reagan will have many battles with. Despite this outward display of strength, Reagan is still struggling to get back to full strength, physically and emotionally – no one knows that he is summoning as much inner strength as he can to deliver the speech if only to assure the country that he is back. He may appear to be back in the saddle, but it becomes clear who will be in control.

Nancy needs to summon as much as she can as well. After the assassination attempt, Nancy Reagan becomes even more protective of her husband, and where this once was a private mission, it has also become a public obsession. She now is on the verge of micromanaging her husband's schedule by working closely with Deputy Chief of Staff Michael Deaver. She is careful to regulate the President's time, fearing that he will be over-scheduled. A very clever woman, she also comes across as manipulative, deluded, and is rumored to become increasingly reliant on fortune tellers. She is well aware that many in America, the press especially, do not like her, especially because of her perceived influence over her husband.

What is clear and unmistakable is that her love and loyalty for Ronald Reagan are absolute. Despite their reliance on astrology, Ronald Reagan surprised his wife one Sunday morning, telling her that they should go to church. Whether this is a result of his near-death experience at the hands of John Hinckley, it is a question that has been left unanswered. Religion had always been a matter of political expediency to Reagan, and the church was never part of the couple's lives. They would need as much help as they can get to go through the crises and problems that are part of being the leader of the free world.

The first domestic "crisis" that Reagan faced occurred just three months later after the assassination attempt on his life.

Reagan announces that the air union representing air traffic controllers in America, Professional Air Traffic Controllers Organization, have left their jobs to strike. Seven months of negotiation between the union and the Federal Aviation Administration have fallen apart, and the union is asking for a 100% increase in pay. Reagan understands that the air traffic controllers' work is crucial to maintaining public safety and national security, but he would not be cowed. He threatened that if the workers do not report for work in 48 hours, all the 13,000 air traffic controllers on strike would be fired. They defy Reagan's ultimatum, confident that the 69-year old's recent assassination attempt would cave in. But they have underestimated the President's resolve, and exactly forty-four hours later, they are all out of a job.

With one swift strike, Ronald Reagan shows that he is strong and very much in charge, even after the assassination attempt. The whole world, especially the Soviet Union, has been put on notice.

Chapter 21

It is April 3, 1982, and Margaret Thatcher, the grocer's daughter, seems to have overlooked her humble origins. As British premiere, her domestic agenda has been comprised mainly of cutting taxes for the wealthy and social programs for the poor. There has been no opportunity for her to show her mettle in foreign policy, and for the most part, has been an unremarkable leader in both international and domestic affairs. Her government is in trouble with the unemployment rate in double digits.

French president François Mitterrand, an ideological opposite, describes Thatcher as having "the eyes of Caligula and the mouth of Marilyn Monroe," alluding to Thatcher's offbeat, and sometimes, cunning look. She has been named, "The Iron Lady," for this countenance, and on this, she must be all that, and more.

Britain's sovereignty has just been challenged by Argentina when its military forces took over the Falklands, a collection of tiny, mountainous islands located in the South Atlantic which had been under British control for 150 years. Thatcher calls Ronald Reagan to ask for U.S. support to retake the Falklands from Argentina, but Reagan refuses. Instead, Reagan suggests that Great Britain give up its claim to the tiny islands, which he says have no strategic or economic value. He says it would help Britain get rid of vestiges of its colonial history. It is a somewhat difficult decision for Reagan, who has to pretend to be neutral. Reagan is a firm backer of Great Britain, and especially Margaret Thatcher, and has in fact very little sympathy or regard for Argentina's arrogant military ruler, General Leopoldo Galtier, whom Reagan considers a drunk.

But Reagan, ever the anti-Communist first, believes that Galtier is a staunch anti-Communist ally, noting the financial and military support he is providing a rebel group, the "Contras," who are revolting against Nicaragua's Marxist regime. Besides, Reagan is still in the formative stages of his own foreign policy, having been in office for just a year. He will not engage the United States in a tiny and inconsequential territorial dispute, with more significant international issues and disputes on his radar: communiques' with the Soviet Union, the crisis between Lebanon and Israel, and the beginnings of a revolt in Soviet-controlled Poland are more urgent concerns.

So now, the Iron Lady must go it alone, and while she appears ill-suited to lead Great Britain to battle, she has no choice but to do it. Thatcher gets the political backing from parliament, and planning for a daring military move to get the islands back, she asks Sir Henry Leach, the head of the Navy, to prepare to attack the Argentines. Three weeks later, on April 25, 1982, Leach leads Royal Marines and British Special forces in an operation that retakes South Georgia Island in the Falklands. Despite this loss, however, the Argentines do not back down. They continue to hold Stanley, the Falklands' main city; and fight back. They sink the British destroyer, Sheffield, the first British ship to be sunk since World War II, and twenty British servicemen die.

With Sheffield's sinking, the world takes notice of the conflict, and Reagan tells an unbelieving Thatcher that once again, the British should leave the Falklands and that the conflict is, "not worth the price." Thatcher does not listen to Reagan, and two weeks later, Stanley finally falls to Great Britain and Argentina withdraws and surrenders. In a matter of weeks, the Iron Lady has earned her sobriquet, while her nation rejoices.

Chapter 22

On the morning of April 15, 1983, Ronald Reagan is talking mental health even as the aging president, just two years into his first term, strains to hear what his speechwriters are saying in their mid-morning meeting. The Oval Office's poor acoustics contribute to the problem. But hearing problems is just one of the issues of old age beginning to manifest itself. Sometimes, while relating a story, he gets lost in the middle of telling it, confusing movie roles with actual events in his life. Regarding being lucid, his own staff admits that he has, "his good days and his bad days."

The *New York Times*, not a friend of Republican presidents, notes that he has a general absent-mindedness about him, forgetting names, making contradictory statements. Other physical signs, such as the nodding of his head, and slight shaking of the hands, are beginning to become more frequent, even if these are not signs of mental illness or impairment by themselves. Previously, the President admitted to journalists that his own mother succumbed to senility and promised that if he should ever be diagnosed with the condition while in office, he will resign from his office.

Ironically, one of the first things Ronald Reagan did when he came into office was to slash federal funding for the treatment of mental illness, while at the same time repealing the Mental Health Systems Act of 1980, and trimming the budget for the National Institute of Mental Health.

In the meantime, a person that truly has mental health issues, John Hinckley, is found not guilty of the charges against him because of insanity. Instead of getting the death penalty and rotting away in solitary confinement in some federal prison, he is assigned to a psychiatric ward in St. Elizabeth's Hospital, a one-hundred-year-old brick mental hospital. Instead of harsh prison life, Hinckley leads a soft life in a minimum security prison.   Inside St. Elizabeth's, he continues to be deluded about Jodie Foster, saying that he sacrificed himself by committing the ultimate crime; all to win Foster's, heart. He wonders if she appreciates what he has done for her. He calls Foster his Josephine to his Napoleon and his Juliet to his Romeo.

Chapter 23

U.S.S.R. is now led by former KGB head Yuri Andropov. The threat of nuclear annihilation is at its highest point in twenty years, as U.S. nuclear missiles in West Germany are pointed at Moscow. Soviet mobile rockets in East Germany are aimed at America's allies in Europe, among them Great Britain. To combat this threat, Thatcher is currently lobbying for American Tomahawk cruise missiles to be based on her island nation.

On March 26, 1983, Margaret Thatcher was entirely furious. The previous day, on Reagan's orders, American troops invaded the former British colony of Grenada, an island in the south Caribbean. On October 19 of the previous year, Marxist commandos overthrew the government, and there were fears that the new Grenadian leaders are aligned with Fidel Castro, and Reagan was forced to act.

Unfortunately, Ronald Reagan never informed the Thatcher government. In fact, his advisers had advised Margaret Thatcher's foreign secretary there would be no attack.

There would be trouble on many fronts this year, not just in Beirut.

Months later, the United States falls victim to a new form of warfare: terrorism. On Sunday morning, October 23, 1983, Beirut, Lebanon, is quiet as the sun rises to the east of the Mediterranean Sea. Outside the barracks of the U.S. Army installation, a yellow Mercedes truck approaches the structure nicknamed the Beirut Hilton from a nearby access road. The truck turns into the parking lot in front of the building. At first, the vehicle appears harmless, even as it proceeds to do a single counterclockwise lap around the lot. Suddenly, the harmless looking truck blows up in an explosion so massive that the FBI will proclaim it to be the biggest nonnuclear bomb in history. 241 American military men are killed in the worst single-day toll since the first day of the Tet Offensive in the Vietnam War, fifteen years before.

Only 6 months earlier, another explosion in Beirut killed 63 people in and around the U.S. embassy.

A few months later, on March 16, 1984, Bill Buckley, an employee in the U.S. Embassy in Iran, is kidnapped and held hostage, but it is only in May when a series of videotapes are sent by the terror group, Hezbollah, that the country learns of the kidnapping and torture of Buckley. He is eventually executed a few years later.

So it is that after three years in office, the president of the United States has had many successes: he has turned around the economy, bringing an end to the recession and reducing the level of unemployment; he has countered the Soviet threat in Europe by placing attack cruise missiles in Germany and England; and, simultaneously, he has begun urging the Soviets to join him in efforts to reduce the possibility of nuclear war through voluntary arms control. Now, he faces the emerging threat of Muslim terrorism.

And if all that isn't enough, Ronald Reagan must now begin another exhausting undertaking: getting reelected.

Chapter 24

It was a warm noon afternoon in August 1984, and Ronald Reagan stands alongside Nancy around their round leather patio table. He is about to perform one of his least-liked tasks as president – he must talk to the media. It is an election year, and the Republican National Convention in Dallas is just three weeks away. Ronald Reagan is not worried about this impromptu news conference since he is never more relaxed than when here at the ranch. Congress is not in session, and he and Nancy are supposed to be relaxing. However, for some reason, Reagan snapped at his wife several minutes before the news conference, ordering her to get out of their limousine.

The press conference is designed to be short and sweet, with only eight questions allowed to be asked by the press. Things go easy at first, with Reagan easily responding to softball questions.

When it is ABC newsman Sam Donaldson's turn, there are suddenly fireworks on this nice, sunny California day. Donaldson has been outwardly provoking, often yelling out questions. He has called Nancy a "smiling mamba," in previous comments, comparing her to the venomous reptile. He curtly asks Reagan about a nuclear arms talk being planned for Vienna and whether Russian leaders will even bother to sit down with the U.S.

In full confrontational mode, he snaps at Reagan, "Is there anything you can do to get them there?"

Taken aback by the question, Reagan mutters, "What?"

Donaldson bellows again, "Is there anything you can do to get them to Vienna?"

Reagan, the polished entertainer who is snappy with his retorts, who has more than had his share of dazzling comebacks, does not have a response. He is in a word, lost.

Nancy Reagan leans over to her husband, and whispers, "We're doing everything we can," to her husband. He repeats this to Donaldson. Nancy has saved the moment.

With Nancy carefully controlling his every appearance, Ronald Reagan hits the campaign trail for real in September. The nation is riveted by his "Morning in America" commercials, which paint a patriotic picture of a country rising from uncertainty and despair.

Yet there is also some unease. Relations between the United

States and the Soviet Union are still very tense, and Reagan has exacerbated the situation by publicly calling the Soviet Union an "Evil Empire.

On September 19, Reagan heads out to New Jersey, and thirty thousand people fill the town square to hear him speak. A large American flag looms over his left shoulder, accompanied by a sign reading, "America: Prouder, Stronger & Better."

Reagan's unlikely speech for today is based on the recent writings of two very prominent conservative voices. The first voice is that of columnist George Will, who behaves decades older than his forty-three years, who surprisingly has become a Bruce Springsteen fan.

At George Will's urging, deputy White House chief of staff Michael Deaver has invited Springsteen himself to the campaign event. But the rocker, having an open date between performances in Philadelphia and Pittsburgh, declines. Ronald Reagan invokes Springsteen's name anyway, his speechwriters mistakenly believing that the song "Born in the U.S.A." is a patriotic anthem. In reality, the opposite is true – its songs vividly depict the loss of homes and jobs for the working poor. The title track, jingoistic in name only, attacks Reagan's economic policies through the eyes of a down-on-his-luck Vietnam vet. At a time when Ronald Reagan wants to appear as if he is in touch, his staff has succeeded in making him look utterly clueless by misinterpreting Springsteen's lyrics.

Three weeks later, Ronald Reagan is confused when about to deliver his closing remarks in the first presidential debate with Walter Mondale. The night has been a catastrophe for Reagan. Walter Mondale was the aggressor throughout the debate, commanding a quick grasp of domestic policy facts and appearing to be more physically robust than Reagan, despite being two inches shorter.

"I wanted to show presidential stature," Mondale will later remember. "I wanted to show mastery of the issues.

Mondale senses a mental weakness in Reagan, afterward telling an aide, "That guy is gone." Despite that, Mondale has refrained from attacking the president in a way that would make Reagan look foolish. Reagan stutters and appears to be a far cry from the man who improvised a brilliant speech within minutes of being called to the podium at the 1976 Republican National Convention.

"I flopped," Reagan says to campaign adviser Stu Spencer immediately upon leaving the stage.

The president is correct. Polls show Walter Mondale winning the debate in a landslide. Two mornings later, the Wall Street Journal will publish a story stating that 10 percent of all people over the age of seventy-five is senile. Reagan is seventy-three years old.

But Ronald Reagan is not finished. He will have one last chance to convince Americans that he is still fit to be their leader. That chance will come on October 21, in Kansas City.

Chapter 25

On October 21, 1984, Ronald Reagan got another shot at Walter Mondale in their second debate in Kansas City.

After the first debate, Nancy Reagan was livid at everyone except at Reagan himself. She excoriated his staff for not having prepared him adequately for the big moment. She warns coldly that they shouldn't do whatever it was they did the first time. She pointed out that Reagan was being bullied during the preparations for the debate, and couldn't respond appropriately because he was always being interrupted. They bring in a new man, Roger Ailes, and the approach to the debate changes drastically.

On the night of the second debate, Reagan seems to have a spring in his step and is more energetic when he grasps the lectern, appearing more poised and confident. He goes through most of the night equipped with more life and energy than from the previous debate.

The Baltimore Sun's Henry Trewhitt, one of those who could query the candidates during the debate, asked straight out if Reagan was too old to continue being president. Reagan, however, had prepared for this moment. During the debate prep, Roger Ailes asked Reagan what his response would be if he were asked if he felt that he was too old for the job. He has the perfect answer which he delivers expertly after Trewhitt asks him the question.

Reagan says casually, as he allows the moment to build up, that he wasn't going to make age an issue in the campaign. Then like the experienced Hollywood hand that he is pauses a bit before delivering the punch line: "I am not going to exploit, for political purposes, my opponent's youth and inexperience." Not yet quite an hour into the debate, Reagan has won it.

On November 6, 1984, Ronald Reagan drubbed Walter Mondale in a historic landslide and was reelected president of the United States. The very next day, Reagan starts a four-day vacation at his ranch, with who else but Nancy.

Chapter 26

December 25, 1986 - Presidential assassin John Hinckley, Jr. has a new love interest. Her name is Leslie deVeau, who, unlike Hinckley, is a real killer; a cold-blooded murderer who killed her own-10-year-old daughter, by shooting her in the back with a shotgun. Hinckley can consider himself lucky. His actions that led to the shooting of Ronald Reagan and three others was considered an act of insanity, sparing him a death penalty and offering him the chance for supervised rehabilitation.

Hinckley and deVeau have been flirting with each other for almost four years, exchanging love notes, smiles, and winks. But on this Christmas day, they get the best chance to consummate their relationship. As everyone is having their Christmas lunch, Hinckley and deVeau sneak into a secluded room and begin making out. Before things get any steamier, however, Hinckley's father barges in, and the rendezvous is over.

Having his parents move east from Colorado is, therefore, a mixed blessing. Letting bygones be bygones, Hinckley's parents have thrown themselves body and soul into their son's recovery. They have sold their house in the home to be closer to their son. They spend every Tuesday afternoon with him, together with a hospital psychiatrist. They entirely invest in his welfare, convinced that a turnaround in their son's mental health is imminent.

Chapter 27

March 1987 – With just a little less than two years left on his last term, Ronald Reagan appears to be losing control of the White House. Four men, Howard Baker, White House counsel, A. B. Culvahouse, director of communications Thomas Griscom, and Washington insider Jim Cannon are in the Oval Office to observe the president.

Nancy Reagan, continuing to rely on astrologers, clashes with new Chief of Staff and former Merrill Lynch head, Don Regan. There is chaos all over the White House as staff decisions seem to be made under Ronald Reagan's nose, including the forging of his initials on documents. Worse, Col. Oliver North appears to have taken advantage of Ronald Reagan's disengagement by funneling the proceeds of arms sales to Iran to anti-communist forces in Latin America, an illegal, impeachable offense if Ronald Reagan put his official stamp of approval on it. It is the stirrings of the Iran Contra scandal that would almost bring down Reagan's presidency. Continuing to protect her husband, Nancy Reagan angrily places all the blame on Don Regan.

The men are not in the Oval Office for just a regular tete-a-tete. They are there primarily to determine if the Twenty-

Fifth Amendment to the Constitution needs to be invoked. The amendment provides for the immediate takeover by of the presidency by the Vice-President if "the president is unable to discharge the powers and duties of his office."

The outward signs are there: the tremors, the forgetfulness, and the lower energy level. At seventy-five, Ronald Reagan is visibly frail, naps frequently, and his eyes project a dull look, sometimes having trouble recognizing people that he has known for years. Nancy Reagan is now his energy surrogate, overriding many White House administrative decisions and beyond. He convinces Donald Regan to fire among others, Margaret Heckler, the secretary of health and human services, Secretary of Labor Ray Donovan, White House communications director Pat Buchanan, and CIA director William Casey. Eventually, an exhausted Regan gives up the fight, and essentially fires himself, replacing himself with Tennessee Senator Howard Baker.

Reagan appears to be revitalized by the shake-up in personnel. The idea of invoking the Twenty-Fifth Amendment is dropped, but Reagan is about to enter an eventful last year of his presidency.

Chapter 28

Ronald Reagan is in trouble.

Wearing a dark blue suit and speckled blue tie, the president prepares to speak to the nation. His face is drawn and lined, with a red flush. His eyes look just to the left of the camera as he reads his message off a teleprompter. He says that he may have approved an arms shipment to the anti-communist forces in Latin American, even if he had denied it earlier.

Many watching the Reagan broadcast know the president has denied committing any illegal acts, but now he seems to be admitting his denial was false.

He says that with the number of meetings and information that passes through his desk every day, he could have missed a memo or two that led to his giving a denial.

The speech is Reagan at his paternal best, letting the nation know that he is still in charge and is managing merely a clerical situation. He diffuses the Iran Contra scandal in one press conference.

In the meantime, Margaret Thatcher, in the midst of a bitter election campaign, is fighting the political battle of her life.

She is in Moscow to meet with the Soviet president, Mikhail Gorbachev. They talk about his recent concessions to the United States to reduce the Soviet Union's arsenal of nuclear weapons. Gorbachev acknowledges that his country faces many problems and he is trying to accomplish this via "perestroika" (restructuring) and "glasnost" (openness). However, he adds that all expectations of change in the Soviet Union must be grounded in "reality," or the world is in great danger, he warns. He also rejects Thatcher's idea that his country still follows a doctrine of communist world domination.

Reagan is unbowed by Gorbachev's underhanded rebuke of Thatcher. He has already assembled the words that will soon astonish the world.

So it is—if not his entire life. On June 12, 1987, Reagan stood before the Berlin Wall where he will give the speech that will define his presidency, having already fully recovered from the Iran-Contra affair. Dapper as ever in his pressed duds, he demands Mikhail Gorbachev, to "tear down this wall."

Chapter 29

It is January 20, 1989, and the last day of Ronald Reagan's presidency. He woke up early to eat his final breakfast in the White House before getting dressed. In a few months, the Berlin Wall that he demanded will be torn down, not by the Russians, but by the sheer force of the democratic forces that he helped unleash in Eastern Europe. The minutes and hours tick by, as the time for his presidency are running out. After tearful goodbyes to his staff, he takes a final walk towards the West Wing, where the new president, George H.W. Bush, will soon call the office his own.

Reagan's final piece of correspondence is a parting letter to his good friend, Margaret Thatcher, who with her husband, became the last foreign dignitary to meet President Reagan. Through their joint efforts, Thatcher and Reagan severely weakened global communism, something once thought impossible. Great Britain's Iron Lady appropriately pointed out that it was Reagan's unwavering belief in American exceptionalism and freedom that inspired the anti-communist revolution to grow and eventually win.

Reagan wishes Bush well, but there is tension between them again as Reagan did very little campaigning for Bush. The distance was caused by Bush generally refusing Reagan's presence, which certainly would have overshadowed him.

Reagan and Nancy are leaving a place that they cherish. Reagan, who cherishes America's traditions has always been moved by the sense of history that the White House exuded. A believer in astrology, he swears the place is haunted by the ghosts of presidents past.

National Security Adviser Colin Powell arrives to provide Reagan's final daily briefing, and a little while later, just before 11:00 a.m., he hands over his plastic authentication card to his air force military aide, constituting his last official act as president of the United States.

At 12:40, with President Bush already having been inaugurated, Ronald and Nancy Reagan step into the Marine helicopter to begin the trip back to California via Andrews Air Force Base.

As they get airborne, Reagan tells Nancy, "Look, honey, there's our little shack."

Chapter 30

On September 8, 1989, White House memories were the least of the things in Ronald Reagan's head. Instead, there is a drill about to enter it as fifty-nine-year-old brain surgeon Dr. Thoralf Sundt, in a procedure called a "burr," presses a surgical bit against the ex-President's head, carefully opening a hole on the right side of his head. The hole, about the size of a nickel, will allow Dr. Sundt to examine the brain in more depth and detail. One burr is enough for him to help diagnose what is wrong with Reagan.

The burr procedure was necessary to evaluate the damage caused by an injury Reagan suffered after he fell off a horse while visiting a friend at his ranch just south of the United States, near the Mexican border. After the accident, he had suffered bouts of dizziness and complained of some pain, while exhibiting increased incidents of forgetfulness. Years later, Nancy Reagan would attribute the hastening of the onset of Reagan's Alzheimer's to the accident.

On February 6, 1993, his closest friends and admirers would get a shocking first-hand view of Ronald Reagan's decline into the disease. To celebrate his 82nd birthday, the Reagans host a huge party for him in California. Reagan proposes a toast for his guest of honor, former British Prime Minister, and dear friend, Margaret Thatcher. It is a heartfelt salute that he is partly reading from a four-page page speech.

Minutes later, Ronald Reagan stands up to deliver another toast to Thatcher. Immediately, shock envelops the room as Ronald Reagan, word for word, delivers the same exact four-page toast to Margaret Thatcher that he uttered just a few moments ago. He continues for two painful minutes in front of a shocked crowd, as the audience, all of them Reagan's friends, sit in stunned silence.

Chapter 31

In June 1994, forty-one-year-old Patti Davis appears in Playboy magazine for the world to see her in all her nude glory. But this is this just the latest shock that Davis will deliver to Ronald and Nancy Reagan. In 1992, Davis published a scathing memoir, exposing unflattering details about her "dysfunctional" family. Among other things, she describes Nancy's reliance of diuretics and tranquilizers, and that Patti herself has led a loose lifestyle that was a polar opposite of the conservative values that her father, and his party, promoted. Patti tells anyone who will listen that it is because of her mother, that she has rebelled, and she maintains that her own mother dislikes her. He father, dismayed at her attitude, personally writes her to assure her that it is not the case. Patti dismisses her father's entreaties.

But family problems are farthest from the mind of Nancy Reagan this year. On April 27, 1994, Ronald and Nancy Reagan are attending the funeral of former President Richard Nixon, who had also lost his wife, Pat just about a year earlier. As Reagan takes his place among the other ex-presidents, the 82-year old is clearly manifesting his age. He is wrinkled, his hair is turning gray, and as Gerald Ford says, he looked "wrinkled out."

Later on that year, Nancy accompanies her husband to the Mayo Clinic for some diagnostic tests. The doctors confirm that Reagan possesses symptoms indicating that he is in the first stages of Alzheimer's disease. The Reagans accept the grim diagnosis and agree that he needs to address the American people, which he has served all his life wholeheartedly.

H writes a heartfelt letter that essentially tells the world that he is facing an incurable disease and that he will be subjecting his family to some hardship. He thanks the country, and asks everyone for their prayers – Ronald Reagan, at 83, is formally exiting his public life.

It is 1996, and it has been two years since Ronald Reagan was diagnosed, and he even forgets that he was once president of the United States. He still keeps regular hours at his office in Century City, mostly reads comics and sits in a nearby park, watching children play.

One morning, his former Secretary of State over his two terms as president, George Shultz, and Nancy are meeting in his office. Reagan sees them and stands to leave the room with his nurse. He turns to nurse and asks her who the man (Schultz) sitting with Nancy is. He tells the nurse that he seems to remember him, and knows that he is a very famous man.

Chapter 32

It is January 20, 2001, almost twenty years to the day when her own beloved Ronnie was being sworn in as President of the United States in the very same place. But now, she is sitting down in a hospital, beside her husband as a new President of the United States, George W. Bush, is being sworn in.

Ronald Reagan, lying down beside her, also watches the ceremony, but unlike her, he has totally forgotten that he took precisely the same oath some twenty years ago back. There is a faraway look in Reagan's eyes that indicates that he is not aware of his current physical condition. Worse for Nancy, he does not even recognize her anymore. He is an obvious shell of his former vigorous, and vibrant, self, unable to feed himself, or even speak. He is just waiting to die.

Patti Davis writes that her mother, "speaks of the loneliness of her life now," noting that while Ronald Reagan is physically present, in many ways, the important ones, he is not.

In a rare interview with Mike Wallace for 60 Minutes, Nancy rues that, "It's lonely," and that, "When you come right down to it, you're in it alone. And there's nothing that anybody can do for you."

On June 5, 2004, with her children surrounding her, she watched her husband slip away, and a just a few moments later, a sobbing Nancy finally acknowledges the reality-Ronald Reagan is gone.

Chapter 33

It is June 11, 2004, and the whole world is mourning, with Ronald Reagan's remains to lie in state at the National Cathedral in Washington, D.C. Margaret Thatcher delivers a mournful eulogy, telling the world that, "We have lost a great president, a great American, and a great man, and I have lost a dear friend." The big screen monitors in the cathedral project her face, and those of others delivering their own eulogies. While most of the world mourns his loss, America's enemies welcome his death. The Communist government in Cuba releases a proclamation stating that Reagan, "Should never have been born." The leftists in America also denigrate him in death, with Christopher Hitchens calling Reagan an, "obvious phony and loon," wondering how America fell for his act.

Like him or not, Reagan's funeral is the biggest one in America since John F. Kennedy was in 1963. Since this is the first national "event" since the 9/11 terrorist attacks, security is extremely tight. However, when the doors are opened after Reagan's body is placed in the Capitol Rotunda, over 100,000 pay their respects, and file his casket to view him for the last time. Margaret Thatcher's eulogy is replayed in the rotunda, and her words cast a solemn spell over those paying their final respects, enunciating Reagan's commitment to serving his beloved America. She said, "Ronald Reagan's life was rich not only in public achievement but also in private happiness. Indeed, his public achievements were rooted in his private happiness."

Despite his scorn for Communism and America's enemies, the inscription on his tombstone reads, "I know in my heart that man is good, that what is right will always eventually triumph, and there is the purpose and worth to each and every life."

But of all the mourners, the saddest person he leaves behind is his wife, Nancy. Reagan acknowledges that the turning point of his life came when he met, and married, Nancy Reagan. Through his divorce, his flings, his career declines, and his defeats, she was there to lift him up. Thatcher recalls Reagan telling her that, "Nancy came along and saved my soul."

Conclusion

There have been a few biographies written about Ronald Reagan that seem to stretch for miles and miles of words and pages. As befitting any historical icon, those books properly give highly pixelated accounts of a man that infuriated enemies, created a cult-like following among admirers, and confounded pundits and political analysts who were sure that he would stumble at some point, at the same time unsure how he got to where he was, and why throngs of people threw in their support for him.

It is somewhat amazing to witness an unassuming bumpkin of a reporter from a small Midwestern college shoot up from nowhere, blaze a searing Hollywood trail as a handsome star, disappears, only to reappear again as a star in another cloth, this time, a star of politics.

In his "second act," the magician behind the curtain seems to be Nancy Reagan, who, aside from being his wife, is Reagan's lieutenant, adviser, consultant, and conscience in all things, even in politics. There are very few people that Reagan shares his life's intimate details with, and Nancy is not only his confessor, but she also screened those who could get close to him. It is not clear how Reagan could have reached the heights of his political career without Nancy Reagan, as it became increasingly difficult in the last twenty years of his life, to divine where Nancy's influence started and ended. She was certainly not the typical First Lady in the background; she was very much the opposite.

Nancy or not, he took the problems of America on his shoulders and led the country through its most difficult economic period since the Great Depression. As if this wasn't enough, he had the world to take care of as well. He ushered it out of the chill of the Cold War, dismantled worldwide Communism, and removed, at least for a while, the threat of global nuclear annihilation.

When a 26-year old Ronald Reagan was mesmerized by the glitz of Hollywood in 1937, he was a preternaturally withdrawn young man who trusted very few people with his innermost thoughts and feelings. He also was sure that while he liked the Hollywood glamor and wanted to be an actor, he probably was not thinking about what it was like to be a star.

It may be said that his political career was following the same template. This time, he wanted to play a big part in changing the fortunes of a state, his country, and the world. That he became a star while doing so seems incidental again. No one really assassinated Ronald Reagan, because he left the world on his own terms. And most importantly, a great majority believed that Ronald Wilson Reagan left the country and the world better places than before he arrived at their grand stages.

FREE BONUSES

P.S. Is it okay if we overdeliver?

Here at Readtrepreneur Publishing, we believe in overdelivering way beyond our reader's expectations. Is it okay if we overdeliver?

Here's the deal, we're going to give you an extremely condensed PDF summary of the book which you've just read and much more...

What's the catch? We need to trust you... You see, we want to overdeliver and in order for us to do that, we've to trust our reader to keep this bonus a secret to themselves? Why? Because we don't want people to be getting our exclusive PDF summaries even without buying our books itself. Unethical, right?

Ok. Are you ready?

Firstly, remember that your book is code: **"READ47"**.

Next, visit this link: **http://bit.ly/exclusivepdfs**

Everything else will be self explanatory after you've visited: **http://bit.ly/exclusivepdfs.**

We hope you'll enjoy our free bonuses as much as we enjoyed preparing it for you!

Summary:

Killing the Rising Sun

By: Bill O' Reilly & Martin Dugard

Proudly Brought to you by:

Legal & Disclaimer

The information contained in this book is not designed to replace or take the place of any form of medicine or professional medical advice. The information in this book has been provided for educational and entertainment purposes only.

The information contained in this book has been compiled from sources deemed reliable, and it is accurate to the best of the Author's knowledge; however, the Author cannot guarantee its accuracy and validity and cannot be held liable for any errors or omissions. Changes are periodically made to this book. You must consult your doctor or get professional medical advice before using any of the suggested remedies, techniques, or information in this book. Images used in this book are not the same as the ones used in the actual book. This is a totally separate and different entity from that of the original book titled: "Killing the Rising Sun"

Upon using the information contained in this book, you agree to hold harmless the Author from and against any damages, costs, and expenses, including any legal fees potentially resulting from the application of any of the information provided by this guide. This disclaimer applies to any damages or injury caused by the use and application, whether directly or indirectly, of any advice or information presented, whether for breach of contract, tort, negligence, personal injury, criminal intent, or under any other cause of action.

You agree to accept all risks of using the information presented inside this book. You need to consult a professional medical practitioner to ensure you are both able and healthy enough to participate in this program.

Table of Contents

The Book at a Glance

This book is about the Second World War and the events that led to the Hiroshima and Nagasaki bombing.

Chapter 1 is about the battle in a small island in Palau called Peleliu, where brave soldiers like Lewis Bausell died.

Chapter 2 is about the highest American military official in the Pacific – Douglas MacArthur and his return to the Philippines.

Chapter 3 is about the man who worked hard to defeat the Japanese – Vice President Harry Truman.

Chapter 4 is about the last days of the battle of Paleliu. In this chapter, you'll find the stories of young American soldiers who sacrificed their lives to win the battle. This chapter also talks about Colonel Nakagawa's death.

Chapter 5 is about the man who considered himself God – Emperor Hirohito of Japan. In this chapter, you'll discover how Hirohito ordered General Yamashita to hold onto the Philippines whatever the cost.

Chapter 6 is about Vice President Truman's piano

performance at a military gathering. This chapter also talks about the Yalta conference attended by the superpowers – President Franklin Roosevelt, President Joseph Stalin, and Prime Minister Winston Churchill.

Chapter 7 is about the battle of Iwo Jima and the liberation of Manila from the Japanese.

Chapter 8 is about the American firebombing operation in Tokyo called Operation Meetinghouse.

Chapter 9 is about President Franklin Roosevelt's death and Harry Truman's inauguration as the new president.

Chapter 10 is about the Manhattan Project and J. Robert Oppenheimer – the father of the atomic bomb. In Chapter 11, you'll read about the battle in Okinawa.

Chapter 12 is about Japan's failed attempt to establish an alliance with Russia. Chapter 13 is about the atomic bomb testing called "Trinity".

Chapter 14 is about the Japanese submarine called I-58. Chapter 15 is about the Potsdam conference, where Truman told Stalin about the atomic bomb.

Chapter 16 is about how the Japanese submarine attacked the USS Indianapolis.

Chapter 17 is about the day America warned the Japanese citizens to evacuate Hiroshima.

In Chapter 18, you'll read about how Colonel Tibbets briefed his teammates about an important mission – the atomic bombing of Hiroshima, Kokuru, and Nagasaki.

In chapter 19, you'll learn how Tibbets dropped the bomb in Hiroshima and in chapter 20 you'll read about how Tibbets' team were getting ready for the second bombing.

In chapter 21, you'll read about the morning after the horrific Hiroshima bombing. Chapter 22 is about how Truman announced the bombing to the citizens of America.

Chapter 23 is about the aftermath of the Hiroshima bombing while chapter 24 is about the bombing in Nagasaki.

Chapter 25 is about Hirohito's decision to surrender to the Americans. Chapter 26 is about the battle between Russia and Japan in Manchuria.

Chapter 26 is about MacArthur's arrival in Japan. Chapter 27 is about the arrest of Japanese war leaders. Chapter 28 is about the meeting between MacArthur and Emperor Hirohito

Chapter 29 is about the execution of the most horrifying

Japanese military leader, Hideki Tojo.

Finally, chapter 30 is about William O'Reilly, the author's father. He was a war veteran who believes that the atomic bombing was a necessary evil to achieve peace.

This book outlines the violence of Japanese soldiers. It's not for the faint of heart.

Dedication

The book is for the war veterans.

Epigraph

"The Land of the Rising Sun" – Chinese description of Japan

A Note To Readers

Five days after the 9/11 attack in New York, Reverend Jeremiah Wright (Barack Obama's pastor) delivered an anti-American statement in his church. He implied that America's sins to the rest of the world justified the attack. The Reverend condemned his own country for blowing up Nagasaki and Hiroshima during World War II.

In 2008, when Senator Barack Obama was vying for the presidency, the media uncovered the pastor's statement. The senator then distanced himself from the pastor, ending their twenty-year friendship.

But, today, not a lot of people know what Wright was talking about. Sure, we know that America dropped an atomic bomb in Hiroshima, but no one knows why. This is the reason why few people would challenge Reverend Wright's statements.

This book is about the horrors of the Second World War. It's about the violent events that eventually led to the Hiroshima and Nagasaki bombing.

This book explains how the United States put an end to the Japanese Empire. This is the sixth book in a series of history books including – Killing Lincoln, Killing Kennedy, Killing Patton, Killing Jesus, and Killing Reagan.

FREE BONUSES

<u>P.S. Is it okay if we overdeliver?</u>

Here at Readtrepreneur Publishing, we believe in overdelivering way beyond our reader's expectations. Is it okay if we overdeliver?

Here's the deal, we're going to give you an extremely condensed PDF summary of the book which you've just read and much more...

What's the catch? We need to trust you... You see, we want to overdeliver and in order for us to do that, we've to trust our reader to keep this bonus a secret to themselves? Why? Because we don't want people to be getting our exclusive PDF summaries even without buying our books itself. Unethical, right?

Ok. Are you ready?

Firstly, remember that your book is code: "**READ48**".

Next, visit this link: **http://bit.ly/exclusivepdfs**

Everything else will be self explanatory after you've visited: **http://bit.ly/exclusivepdfs.**

We hope you'll enjoy our free bonuses as much as we enjoyed preparing it for you!

Introduction

On October 12, 1939, an economist named Alexander Sachs visited President Franklin Roosevelt. It was a top secret meeting and it had been six weeks since the Germans took over Poland. On August 2, Albert Einstein wrote a letter to the president warning him that it's possible to build powerful bombs made of a large mass of uranium. These bombs are powerful enough to blow up cities and the Nazis are in the process of building them. At that time, the Nazis had already taken over the uranium mine in Czechoslovakia.

Einstein wrote an eight hundred word document summarizing America's uranium output at that time. The president asked the economist questions about the new type of bomb.

After the meeting with Sachs, the president called in his secretary – a retired army general named Edwin "Pa" Watson. The president calmly asked Pa to take immediate action.

That's how the age of mass destruction began. The chapters in this book detail the events that led to the destruction of Hiroshima and Nagasaki using the type of bomb that Albert Einstein wrote about.

1

This chapter talks about the legendary battle of Peleliu - the controversial attack that started the demise of Imperial Japan.

Peleliu is a small island in Palau, near the Philippine Sea. The island is just two miles long and six miles wide. Japan took control over the empty island in 1914. The island remained empty and unused for almost twenty years. When World War II started, the Japanese began using the island as a fortress to protect one of their prized treasures from the Americans – the Philippines.

At that time, the Japanese military men in Peleliu were under the command of Colonel Kunio Nakagawa. He was a good war strategist. He built a network of five caves where the elite soldiers hid and waited for the US troops. Japanese soldiers were called "formidable fighting insects", dueto their ability to attack their enemies out of nowhere. These soldiers were well-trained. They've been living in underground tunnels eating rice and fish. Their commanders would punish and beat them for just about anything – for being too tal or too short. They were hardened by years of battle and harsh discipline.

The strength of the Japanese soldier was their willingness to die. They thought that surrendering to the enemy was a deep form of dishonor. They would rather die than live as a prisoner.

On September 15, 1944, the American soldiers landed in the shore of Peleliu. Marine Corps Colonel Lewis Puller ordered his team to take no prisoners and kill every Japanese soldier.

Corporal Lewis Kenneth Bausell was one of the US marine soldiers tasked to take over Peleliu. He was only 21 years old and a bookbinder from Washington, DC. He was in his freshman year in McKinley Technical High School when the Japanese attacked Pearl Harbor. So, he decided to join the Marines. During his two years of service being a marine, he earned the respect of his peers and colleagues. He did well during the American invasions in Gavutu, Tulagi, Cape Gloucester, and Guadalcanal. He was a good fighter and was promoted to sergeant.

Colonel Bausell kept his head down as they hit the beach. Japanese snipers could be just around the corner. The Japanese soldiers launched a number of 141mm mortar towards the ship, killing a number of marines. Peleliu is a tropical paradise, but it was a living hell that day. The palm trees were burning and the beach was filled with blood.

Bausell told the soldiers to hit the beach. The soldiers were praying hard for survival.

Peleliu was not easy to conquer. The mortar launchers and artillery were hidden behind the beachfront. The Japanese also constructed hundreds of mines. The beach was protected with barb wire and they built machine gun nests called Spider Traps. These weapon nests were made of coconut logs so they blended well with the island's tropical landscape. It was hard for American soldiers to spot these machine gun nests.

Colonel Nakagawa knew that the US force was huge. So, he employed a clever strategy – employing a few soldiers on the beaches, while thousands of soldiers hid in the caves near the Umurbrogol Highlands.

Private Dan Lawler, one of the American marine soldiers, later said that the US Troops were determined to kill or be killed. These soldiers knew how cruel the Japanese were. They have seen bodies of fallen American soldiers tied to a tree. Some had their legs, heads, or arms chopped off. It was horrifying.

Colonel Bausell and his men started to fire into a small cave opening. Lt. Jack Kimble and two other soldiers threw a stream of fire into the cave, hoping that this would force the

Japanese troops to come out.

The first Japanese to come out were carrying a grenade. Bausell shot him. Then, another soldier came out. Lt. Jack Kimble and his flamethrowers turned the soldier into a human torch. But the grenade was already in plain view. Bausell threw himself onto the grenade to protect other soldiers. He was heavily injured. On September 18, Lewis Bausell died. He was the first US marine to receive the highest award for courage and valor – the Medal of Honor, but he's not the last.

The battle of Peleliu lasted for 13 days, but, on October 20, the American forces had already gained enough momentum and the troops were getting ready to liberate the Philippines from Japan.

In the next chapter, you will learn about General Douglas McArthur's determination to liberate the Philippines from the Japanese.

This chapter talks about General McArthur's mission to liberate one of the biggest Japanese territories during World War II – the Philippines.

General Douglas McArthur played an important role in killing the Rising Sun and defeating the Japanese empire. He was over six feet tall and was the son of a war hero – Arthur McArthur Jr. His father fought in the American-Spanish War and became the military governor of the Philippines. He was also the recipient of the Medal of Honor.

Douglas studied at West Point. He graduated top of his class in 1903 and started his military career the same year.

McArthur became the United States army commander in the Far East in 1941. He was tasked to protect the Philippines from a Japanese invasion, but he failed. On December 7, 1941, the Japanese attacked a ship at Pearl Harbor. On that day, US declared war against Japan and its closest ally – Germany. The next day, the Japanese attacked the American base in Clark, Philippines. Two days later, the Japanese dropped bombs in Cavite. The attacks were well-planned. There were hundreds of spies deployed in the Philippines. In fact, the president of the Philippines, Manuel L. Quezon would later remember that his masseur and gardener were both Japanese.

In the next two months, the Japanese forces continued to move and take control of major cities in the Philippines. In 1942, McArthur and his team were forced to hide in Bataan. They were called the "Bataan Gang", but Bataan also fell into the hands of the Japanese. The Bataan Gang was forced to escape to Australia but McArthur promised that he would return and free the Philippines from the Japanese regime. This was the most humiliating defeat in his entire career. McArthur is known for his huge ego and the fall of the Philippines was a devastating, ego-crushing experience. But it was not all bad. That same year, Douglas McArthur was awarded the Medal of Honor for his strong leadership and heroism in the Philippines. This made Douglas and Arthur, the first father-son tandem to receive the Medal of Honor in America. Even after he was given the medal, McArthur vowed to take back the Pacific from the hands of the enemies.

On October 20, 1944, the "A-day" or "Attack Day", McArthur arrived in Red Beach, Leyte, Philippines. McArthur went down the ladder of the ship. The rest of the "Bataan Gang" got out of the ship. It was a huge PR stint. The American forces brought a team of photographers to capture the moment. McArthur had fulfilled his promise. He had returned.

McArthur knew that his return to the Philippines played a vital role in defeating Japan. It was the greatest oceanic landing in history. McArthur said: "Filipino people, I have returned".

In the next chapter, we will discuss America's political climate amidst the war.

In this chapter, we will discuss how future president Harry Truman geared to help President Franklin Roosevelt secure his fourth term.

Harry Truman believed that he was already immune to the mudslinging associated with politics. But the sixty-year old vice presidential candidate was still considered a newbie in American politics.

He was working hard to make himself known. He delivered the best speeches. But, despite his efforts, his appearances did not make it to the front pages of the newspapers. Most journalists opted to cover World War II. Thousands of marines were either wounded or killed in Peleliu. The fight for control over the Philippines was also not easy. McArthur's troops were attacked by the Japanese suicide pilots called kamikaze. Japanese soldiers were determined to stay in control of the Philippines.

Despite the lack of media coverage, Truman was confident that Roosevelt's popularity and his stern leadership during World War II would secure the victory of the Democratic Party. America loved Roosevelt.

Roosevelt was popular, but Harry Truman was relatively unknown and unpopular. There were even rumors that he was part of the White Supremacist group called Ku Klux Klan. Good thing that the leader of black groups came forward to defend him.

On November 3, 1944, Truman arrived in his hometown Kansas City with his family, after campaigning in other cities. The family decided to stay at the Muehlebach Hotel. It was one of the most popular hotels in the state. Babe Ruth, Bob Hope, and Helen Keller had stayed there. Harry Truman carried his own suitcase. He even washed his own socks. That's how different he was from Douglas McArthur, who had not carried his own baggage, or opened the door for years. Harry Truman was humble and pleasant.

As he went to his room, Truman thought he could finally rest. He was wrong. The next chapter talks about the last days of the Battle of Peleliu.

This chapter talks about the last days of the Battle of Peleliu and the fall of Colonel Nakagawa.

The US marines fought bravely at Peleliu. They were all prepared to die for their country. Corporal Bausell was the first soldier to give his life to save other soldiers. After a few days, seven other soldiers were awarded the Medal of Honor for displaying courage. Four other soldiers threw themselves on grenades to save their comrades.

On September 18, the same day Bausell died, Private First Class Arthur Jackson attacked a cement box containing 35 Japanese soldiers. He fired his M1 into the small opening and threw grenades into the bunker, killing all thirty five enemies.

But Jackson was not finished yet. The 19-year old soldier savagely shot every Japanese soldier he could see. He wiped out a total of twelve caves, killing another fifty enemies. This one-man offensive came to an end when Jackson collapsed from heat exhaustion. But he lived to tell his story.

On September 19, the Company Corps commander, Captain Everett Pope, showed bravery as well. Pope was a loving husband and father of two children. But he was also a highly skilled killer and military leader. On that day, he was ordered to take Hill 154, also known as the "Suicide Ridge". Pope and his team were already tired. Most of his men had died. They were thirsty and hungry. Many of the soldiers did not wear underwear because of heat.

As Pope and his team approached Hill 154, the Japanese soldiers popped out of nowhere and fired shots. Afterwards, they retreated to their caves again. Pope's men ran, but they returned to the hill in the middle of the night. Japanese and American soldiers fought until dawn. The next day, Pope and his team stood on the hill. They had successfully taken the Suicide Ridge.

The fight for Hill 154 had set the tone of the entire combat for Peleliu – the American soldiers attacked the fortresses and then, the Japanese went out of their caves to fight back. American F4U Corsair fighter bombers would regularly bomb the mountain ridges of Umurbrogol Pocket. But there was one problem. The Japanese soldiers were not on the island, they were living underground. American soldiers were persistent and, cave by cave, they slowly took control the entire Umurbrogol Mountain. It was not easy, though. It took one thousand five hundred bullets to kill one Japanese soldier. Nakagawa's war tactic has cost the lives of fifteen thousand soldiers.

Colonel Kunio Nakagawa was one of the bravest Japanese military leaders. He killed or wounded more than ten thousand American soldiers. He was considered one of the greatest Japanese fighters. He was also a great strategist. He built an underground fortress where his soldiers hid. In the middle of the night, Nakagawa's soldiers would leave the caves and kill American soldiers while they were asleep.

On November 24, Nakagawa realized that he had lost the war. His superior, Major General Kenjiro Murai, decided to perform Seppuku, or ritual suicide. As General Murai's kaishakunin (second in command), Nakagawa was tasked to assist Murai in committing suicide.

Murai knelt down and plunged the sword to his stomach, spilling his intestines. He fell forward and died after 30 seconds. Nagawa knelt down beside Murai's dead body, praying for the courage to die with honor. Finally, he plunged a sword to his stomach.

It was a victory for America, but war strategists could not help but ask. If thousands of soldiers died in a fight over a small island, how many American soldiers would have to die to invade Japan?

The next chapter is about the man who called himself God – Emperor Hirohito. The next chapter also talks about how Japanese soldiers destroyed and raped the entire city of Nanking.

On November 24, 1944, Colonel Nakagawa performed ritual suicide (seppuku, popularly known as harakiri). It was the beginning of the end of the Japanese empire.

World War II officially began when Germany invaded Poland in September 1, 1939, but the first act of aggression began two years before, when Japan conquered a Chinese province called Manchuria.

In December 1939, the Japanese captured the city of Nanking. Japanese soldiers went on killing sprees. They ignored the agreement of the Geneva Conventions, which protected prisoners of war from execution, assault, or torture. Japanese soldiers were savage. Chinese people were beheaded, buried alive, or attacked by dogs.These barbaric acts were, however, only prelude to what would happen to the women of Nanking.

About eighty thousand women in Nanking were systematically raped. Japanese soldiers would later say how much they enjoyed these acts. They even forced brothers to rape their sisters and sons to rape their mothers. The victims were killed after they were raped, but the women who survived became sex slaves called "comfort women". The Japanese soldiers murdered half of the residents of Nanking – that was around three thousand people.

President Franklin Roosevelt did not believe the "rape of Nanking" at first. He dismissed it as an urban legend. Because of that, the American government stayed silent and did not do anything to help the people of Nanking.

But the Japanese continued to expand their territory. Japan was not rich in natural resources, so they needed to conquer countries that were, such as the Philippines, China, Malaysia, Burma, and Indonesia.

So, on July 26, 1941, President Roosevelt froze all the Japanese assets in the US to stop Japan's aggression in Asia. The US confiscated Japan's oil tanks. The Japanese military generals saw this move as an act of aggression. Japan went on to invade every country and island where they could extract oil and other natural resources.

Japan's prime minister at that time was Fumimaro Konoe, who was known for his peace-loving nature. He hoped to come up with a diplomatic agreement with the United States. But when he knew that it was impossible to get a peace treaty, he resigned. He could not stomach all the brutality of the war.

Konoe was replaced by an arrogant army leader named Hideki Tojo. He was known as Razor because of his intense attention to detail. As prime minister, he was the second most popular person in Japan. Tojo orchestrated the war. He persuaded the Emperor to conquer various territories in Asia and the Pacific. He was the mastermind of the Pearl Harbor attack. During the war, the Emperor made Tojo the face of Japan.

Colonel Nakagawa died on Thanksgiving day – November 24, 1944. In Japan, Nakagawa's God, Emperor Michinomiya Hirohito, was eating vegetables and dumpling soup. He believed that he was a God, the descendant of a Shinto sun goddess named Amaterasu.

But Hirohito did not look like a God. He was short and shy. His life was quite ordinary. He lived in a large castle, but he did not drink wine or smoke cigars. He also had a number of worries that kept him up at night. He knew that there were thousands of people who wanted to destroy him.

He waked up at 7 am and ate bread and oatmeal. He was married to a distant cousin and had seven children. He was nearsighted and only stood 5'5". He was the smallest war leader in the world. The Japanese people loved him, although they rarely saw him. The Emperor rarely went out of his castle. He did not deliver speeches. All his proclamations were printed, so a lot of Japanese soldiers did not even know what he looked like. But most of these soldiers were willing to die for the unseen Emperor.

Hirohito allowed his military leaders to strategize and conduct the war. In 1937, the Emperor said he was satisfied when the Japanese soldiers killed thousands of people in Nanking, China. He also did not stop his military generals from attacking Pearl Harbor and waging war against the United States.

As he ate his lunch on November 24, he sent an order to General Tomoyuki Yamashita to hold on to the Philippines at all cost. The Emperor considered that their victory over the Americans in the battle of Leyte was the biggest military achievement of Japan since 1582.

The emperor was worried. He knew that the Philippines would eventually fall into the hands of the Americans, but he would do everything he could to stop it. He armed the ordinary citizens of Japan. All schools and companies were required to conduct military training for their students and employees. Hirohito was actively involved in developing sure victory weapons. He was a great strategist.

On November 24, he knew that a lot of his soldiers were destroyed. A number of Japanese vessels were destroyed. He knew that he was losing the war, but he refused to seek peace. He chose to fight until death.

On February 10, 1945 at around 8:30 pm, around eight hundred military men cheered, as Vice President Harry Truman sat at the piano in the ballroom of the National Press Club. But he was not the only celebrity guest that night. A young sex symbol named Lauren Bacall sat on top of the piano, posing for the cameras, while Truman played.

President Roosevelt ignored Truman after they won the election. But the Vice President did not care. He was just happy to preside over the senate and deliver ceremonial speeches. He had played the piano since he was ten years old and he was happy to play for the brave American soldiers.

Days earlier, the Yalta conference began after the defeat of the Nazis. The conference was held at the Yusupov, Livadia, Vorontsov, and Yusupov Palaces in Yalta, Crimea, Soviet Union.

President Franklin Roosevelt was already sick and dying, but he traveled to Russia just to meet with other world leaders.

The big three —Franklin Roosevelt, Wilson Churchill, and Joseph Stalin- all attended the conference. These leaders were determined to define the post-war world.

It was no secret that Joseph Stalin was a cunning man. He bugged the American president's room. Roosevelt's servants were Russian spies. Stalin was determined to get Churchill and Roosevelt to help him restore the same shape and size of the pre-war Russian empire. But there was one territory that he wanted to occupy – Manchuria. Russia and Japan fought for this territory in 1904. The Russian lost, but Stalin was determined to have his revenge.

Stalin agreed to fight Japan in exchange of the control over Manchuria. After the conference, the three leaders agreed that the rest of the world would be divided between the Soviet Union and the United States. Great Britain came out as the biggest loser as most of its former territories were seeking independence. Roosevelt was okay with the whole arrangement. He believed that he could trust Joseph Stalin. But what he did not know was that he had just consigned a number of European nations to years of Russian communist occupation.

On February 10, a team of scientists were in a laboratory in a desert near Manzanar. They were laying down the final design of a new weapon they called "atom bomb". America intended to use this weapon against Germany, but since they were already defeated, this weapon would be used against Japan.

The weapon was still untested, but if all went well, B-29 bombers launching from the Pacific Islands would drop these bombs in Japan. The explosive effect of this new weapon was equal to 10 kilotons of ordinary dynamite. General Leslie Groves planned to drop these bombs in Kyoto, Kokura, Hiroshima, Niigata, and Yokohama. The scientists code-named the weapon "Little Boy". This name was inspired by the film of Lauren Bacall's fiancé – The Maltese Falcon.

Lauren Bacall's appearance with Harry Truman on February 10, 1945 had a historical significance after all.

The next chapter is about the battle for the control of Manila, the Capital of the Philippines, and a small island near mainland Japan called Iwo Jima.

On February 19, 1945, "Manila John" Basilone was on an island called Iwo Jima (Codename: Island X).

Iwo Jima is a small Japanese volcanic island that is located between mainland Japan and the Philippines.

Manila John Basilone was twenty years old. He was a boxer and a decorated war hero who fought bravely in the Philippines in 1942. After fighting numerous battles, he toured around the United States to sell war bonds. But he knew that he was ready to return to the battle field.

Basilone and his team pressed their bodies on the sand as bullets flew around. Many soldiers died, but Basilone led some of the marines forward. The soldiers were tired, but they were determined to take Iwo Jima, even if it would cost them their lives.

Basilone was a newlywed at that time. He had everything to live for. But he fought like he had nothing to lose.

He attacked the Japanese pillboxes as if he was bulletproof. On that day, February 19, 1945, John "Manila John" Basilone died. In a period of five weeks, a total of six thousand

American soldiers and twenty-one Japanese soldiers also died. But the war was far from over.

On February 22, 1945 at 11 am, Douglas McArthur was at the Penthouse Apartment of the Manila Hotel. His seven year old son Arthur and his wife Jean were living in Brisbane at that moment. But they would be returning to the Philippines soon.

McArthur and his family once lived in this lavish penthouse apartment but it was now ruined. The Japanese used the apartment as a command post and they burned it as the American soldiers entered the building.

General McArthur left the burned luxury apartment with the Thirty-Seventh division of the US army. Their machine gun barrels were still hot. He felt sad for the people of Manila who lost their homes and dignity.

The battle for Manila began on February 3, 1945. McArthur prematurely announced to the American press that Manila had fallen. But this was not true. Even though General Yamashita had ordered his men to evacuate the city, there were still a number of rogue Japanese soldiers who refused to obey the general's orders.

These Japanese soldiers hid in houses and shoot all American soldiers they could see. For two weeks, Manila was not a safe place.

After two weeks, the Japanese soldiers realized that they were losing the battle. But even when they were losing, they still thought that their race was superior to the Filipinos'. So, they killed and defiled as many Filipinos as they could, before they died. They beheaded many Filipinos and raped hundreds of Filipinas.

But, as McArthur stood in front of the penthouse apartment, he knew that he would be liberating the Filipinos from Japanese soldiers' cruelty soon.

On March 4, 1945, Manila was officially liberated from the Japanese. Two days after, the SS British Columbia Express arrived in Manila. General Douglas McArthur rode a small boat to meet the ship. His wife and son had arrived.

On March 9, 1945, B-26 aircrafts departed from American bases in Saipan and Taiwan to the capital city of Japan - Tokyo. These planes contained M-69 firebombs. The Americans were determined to execute Operation Meetinghouse, which turned out to be one of the most horrifying bombings in the world.

The B-26 aircrafts were under the command of a thirty-eight year old commander named General Curtis LeMay. He was a skilled pilot. Many people considered him heartless and brutal, but many soldiers respected him for his tactical brilliance. He ordered his men to burn down Tokyo and wipe it off the map. The goal was to crush the will and the spirit of the Japanese people.

On March 10, 1945, American M-69 bombs were flying around Tokyo. At around 12:08 am, most residents were still awake. They ran through the city streets, desperate to save their life. Most of them hid on anything that could protect them from the flying bombs. Many Japanese people dug out holes. It was a holocaust.

The M-69 firebombs were different from the untested atomic

bombs developed at Los Alamos, Mexico, but they were equally deadly. One M-69 bomb could start a fire. A ton of these bombs could destroy a village.

In the morning of March 10, the B29 planes dropped two thousand tons of M-69 bombs on the city of Tokyo. The bomb bay doors opened at 1 am and Tokyo was on fire 14 minutes later.

On March 18, the great and arrogant Emperor Hirohito toured around the burned-down areas of Tokyo. He went out of his maroon Rolls-Royce and saw tired and devastated Japanese citizens living in their ruined homes.

General LeMay repeated the same firebombing attack in other Japanese cities – Kawasaki, Kobe, Osaka, Yokohama, and Nagoya. After two weeks, the firebombing ended because the pilots were exhausted and the planes ran out of M-69s, after dropping five million firebombs in Japan.

The next chapter is about the day Harry Truman was sworn as the President of the United States.

On April 12, 1945, Vice President Harry Truman was in Room H-128 of the capital building. Congressman Rayburn, the speaker of the House, told him to call White House Press Secretary Steve Early immediately.

Truman stopped for a moment. The calls from the White House were rare. He picked up the phone and dialed the number of the press secretary.

"This is VP", Truman said. The press secretary instructed the Vice President to come to the White House quietly and quickly.

When Truman arrived at the White House, Eleanor Roosevelt approached him saying that her husband had died earlier that day.

On that day, Truman was sworn in as the new president of the United States. On April 24, the new president was briefed that America would soon test a new weapon called the Atomic Bomb. Only the president could make the final decision of dropping this powerful bomb, although President Truman did not know where the bomb was. This weapon would end the Pacific war. The next day, the president authorized the invasion of Japan. He knew that eventually he would have to use the bomb to crush Japan.

10

On April 22, 1945, a brilliant but eccentric physicist named J. Robert Oppenheimer celebrated his birthday in a large cottage in Los Alamos, New Mexico. His guests included chemists, physicists, and Nobel Prize winners. Oppenheimer was considered as the most dangerous person in the world at that time. He was the father of the atomic bomb.

Everyone in the cottage had top secret clearance so they could talk freely about the atomic bomb. Half of the guests believed that it was okay to drop the bomb in Japan, while the rest thought that it was morally wrong to destroy a country that was about to surrender.

After drinking the night away, Oppenheimer woke up before 7:30 am the next day to head to work at the bomb factory.

It had been six years since Franklin Roosevelt and Alexander Sachs first talked about the atomic bomb.

Three years before, Brigadier General Leslie Groves asked Oppenheimer to build a state of the art laboratory in the middle of the desert. The physicist convinced some of the world's most brilliant minds to join him.

Oppenheimer was eccentric and he had a long history of depression, but he was a genius. The government purchased an old school called Los Alamos and transformed it into a laboratory. The building was surrounded by barb wires, attack dogs, and military guards. In 1945, Oppenheimer was extremely stressed. He had lost a lot of weight and he rarely ate.

His wife, a genius named Kitty Oppenheimer, went to live with her parents. Kitty took their four-year old son, but left their four-month old baby with a friend. While Kitty was away, Oppenheimer developed sexual affairs with various women.

Oppenheimer graduated from Harvard with flying colors. He had a PhD in Physics from the University of Gottingen in Germany. He believed in Eastern philosophy. He called the atomic bomb test "Trinity" after the three Hindu gods – Vishnu, Shiva, and Brahma.

Oppenheimer was a walking contradiction, but he knew that he was the real-life Grim Reaper.

The next chapter talks about the battle of Okinawa.

Adolf Hitler and his wife killed themselves on April 30, 1945. After seven days, the Germans issued unconditional surrender. News of Hitler's death traveled across the globe. On May 8, 1945, the marines tasked to conquer Japan heard about Hitler's tragic death, but they could not care less. They were tasked to conquer Okinawa.

Okinawa was an island filled with Japanese and Chinese farmers. A number of these citizens committed suicide to avoid falling into the hands of the American soldiers.

Moments before assaulting a five mile cliff in Okinawa called Maeda Escarpment, Private First Class Desmond Doss asked his commander, Lieutenant Cecil Gornto, if he could pray. The commander nodded, so the young soldier started to pray.

Doss was the company medic and a devout Seventh Day Adventist. He did not eat pork, drink, or work on Saturdays. He refused to carry firearms during battles. His behavior was considered eccentric and many soldiers thought that he was mentally unbalanced. But he ignored all the accusations and became a hero in the battles for Leyte (Philippines) and Guam.

After saying a prayer, Doss' teammates said "amen". It was already dawn and the soldiers were getting ready to reach the peak of the Maeda Escarpment without detection.

May 13 was a Saturday and was supposed to be a time for rest and prayer. But Doss continued to tend to the fallen soldiers. He brought down every fallen soldier (dead or alive) from the Maeda Escarpment. Japanese soldiers tried to shoot Doss, but missed. The young medic singlehandedly saved 75 soldiers.

The Japanese soldiers fought in Okinawa for more than two months. On January 23, 1945, the Americans officially won the Battle of Okinawa thanks to men like Doss.

Japan's citizens were bleeding. Most cities were on fire. But Hirohito still refused to surrender. The age of atomic bombing would begin 44 days after the Battle of Okinawa ended.

On January 24, 1945, former Japanese Prime minister Koki Hirota was at Gora Hotel, in Hakone, to meet with Yakov Malik, the Soviet Union ambassador to Japan.

Koki Hirota was 67 years old at that time. He was a diplomat and a skilled negotiator. He was a thin man with a moustache. The fall of Okinawa made Emperor Hirohito desperate, so he authorized Hirota to talk to Malik on his behalf.

The British and the Americans publicly said that the Second World War was not over until the Axis Powers (Germany, Italy, and Japan) were crushed. So, Hirota asked Russia to convince Britain and the US that unconditional surrender was not necessary. At this point, Japan just wanted to stop fighting.

But Yakov Malik was clear that peace did not depend on Russia. He refused to directly answer Hirota's request and Hirota returned to Tokyo. He knew that Russia would never help Japan.

At this point, it was already clear that both Hirota and the Imperial Japan would eventually die and pay for their sins.

The next chapter talks about the atomic bomb testing known as the "Trinity".

On July 16, 1945 at around 1 am, Robert Oppenheimer paced in his room in Alamogordo, New Mexico. The atomic bomb testing called the "Trinity" would happen in less than three hours. Oppenheimer was nervous.

General Leslie Groves, the chief executive of the Manhattan Project, arrived. He wanted the test to push through despite of the bad weather. At that time, President Harry Truman was at a summit with Winston Churchill and Joseph Stalin. Oppenheimer had convinced the general to postpone the test, but only for an hour.

Robert Oppenheimer was nervous. His engineers promised that that the test would be successful, but he bet ten dollars that the bomb would not detonate. The test was successful.

Because of the successful test, the scientists built two other atomic bombs and shipped one of them to the Pacific. Oppenheimer and his team discovered that the bomb would shoot up to over 40,000 feet. The heat melted the desert sand into green glass. This material was soon called the "trinitite".

The test was confidential, but many people noticed the

explosion. It was almost like an earthquake. At 8pm on July 16, President Truman received a telegram announcing the success of the test. Truman's reaction was guarded.

Oppenheimer had a different reaction. He knew that he built something that was extremely terrifying and could kill thousands of people.

On July 14, 1945, eight Japanese ferries in Hokkaido sunk, killing a lot of people. The Americans attacked these ships to prevent the Japanese soldiers from shipping coal from Hokkaido to Japanese bomb, gun, and airplane factories.

On July 16, 1945 at around 4 pm, the Japanese submarine called I-58 departed from the port of Kure. It was loaded with one month worth of fuel, food, and torpedoes. The submarine was under the command of Lieutenant Mochitshura Hamimoto.

Many Japanese cities had been destroyed by the US Air Forces. The US Navy also launched various aerial attacks.

Naval aviators were now flying all day, destroying Japan's ships, ports, railways, and aerial defenses. The Americans were slowly destroying Japan's confidence and morale. The Japanese people were extremely hungry and humiliated. Citizens were ordered to use the Ketsu-Go (suicide) strategy. This meant that all men, children, and women should fight the American soldiers until death. But, by this time, it was too late for Ketsu-go. The citizens' weapons were destroyed. Japan was almost on life support.

Despite all the devastation and the humiliation, Mochitsura Hamimoto still ran the best and most powerful submarines in the world. The vessel was more than three hundred feet long and about thirty feet wide. I-58 was bigger than most American submarines and more powerful, too. But it had not destroyed an American ship yet.

Hashimoto was a thirty-year old soldier and the son of a Shinto priest. He prayed that an American ship soon hit one of his submarine's torpedoes. His prayer would soon get an answer.

The next chapter is about the Potsdam Conference in Germany, where Truman told his allies about his plan to drop the atomic bomb in Japan.

On July 25, 1945, President Truman was in a room in Potsdam, Germany. He missed his wife dearly. He was bothered by the fact that American now owned a powerful war weapon that could destroy thousands of lives.

President Truman wrote in his journal that the deadly weapon was going to be used on August 10 to attack Hiroshima's 350,0000 residents. Most of the city's residents were marines and soldiers. The city's port was also the largest military supply depots in Japan.

Earlier that day, Truman attended the Potsdam Conference summit meeting with Winston Churchill and Joseph Stalin. It was the first time Truman met Joseph Stalin in person. At that time, Truman had not told his allies about the atomic bomb that he planned to drop in Hiroshima.

After the meeting, Truman quietly walked to Stalin and told him that America had a new powerful weapon that could destroy Japan.

Stalin said through an interpreter that he was glad to hear the news. But Stalin already knew about the atomic bomb. He had spies in Los Alamos. Stalin was calm as he walked away from Truman. But the truth was, he was nervous. The Russian president wanted to dominate the world and he knew that America's new weapon could prevent him from doing that.

The next chapter is about the planning of the Operation Olympic.

On July 30, 1945, McArthur was in office in the Manila City Hall, waiting for the arrival of Vice Admiral Ross T. McIntire and H. Struve Hensel (Assistant Secretary of the Navy).

McArthur was the most senior military officer and the most powerful man in the Pacific. He had served eight presidents and was awarded the Medal of Honor. But he did not know anything about the atomic bomb in Los Alamos.

MacArthur's men continued to prepare for the eventual invasion of Japan, but MacArthur spent his days talking to reporters and entertaining American guests at his mansion called Casa Blanca. It was a big and luxurious house that stood strong amidst the destroyed homes of Manila. McArthur lived an extravagant life with his wife and son.

Vice Admiral Ross McIntire and H. Struve Hensel arrived in the Manila City Hall. MacArthur sat with these military leaders and discussed the influx of Japanese forces in Kyushu. The meeting lasted for 30 minutes.

MacArthur had been planning the invasion of Kyushu for a while now. The mission was called Operation Olympic and was scheduled for November 1, 1945. While reading the report handed by the two military leaders, MacArthur realized that the Japanese soldiers were adopting a new strategy. They no longer hid in caves and waited for American soldiers to attack. MacArthur realized that the Japanese would defend the Kyushu beaches with intense passion and determination.

That day, MacArthur thought that there were only three ways to defeat Japan in Kyushu:

Initiate a naval blockade, followed by an invasion;

Invade the beaches straight up;

Naval blockade and aerial bombing.

Even when the Americans were already winning, the Japanese forces were still determined to kill their enemies. The evidence of Japan's persistence to kill American soldiers lied 160 feet deep in the Pacific Ocean, about 600 miles away from Manila – the I-58.

Hashimoto strategically placed his submarine in the middle of the most common shipping lane between the Philippines and Guam.

On July 29, Hashimoto tried to attack an American cargo ship called the Wild Hunter. The ship was fully armed, so the submarine failed to destroy it. This missed opportunity made Hashimoto the target of the American navy.

Hashimoto's vessel was running out of food and fuel. He was getting desperate to kill American soldiers and destroy ships.

At that time, the USS Indianapolis was just 13 miles away from the I-58. This ship was under the command of Captain Charles McVay.

As the US ship approached the submarine, Hashimoto ordered his men to load six "Type 95" torpedoes.

Hashimoto scanned the horizon and was pleasantly surprised to see that his target ship did not have an escort. It was basically unarmed.

Hashimoto waited patiently until his vessel was at 60-foot depth. When the time was right, the Japanese commander ordered his men to shoot up the torpedoes. The American ship was sinking fast.

McVay ordered his men to abandon the ship, determined to save his staff. Many sailors jumped into the water without life jackets.

Out of the 1,196 people, 800 made it into the sea. Then the sharks arrived, but most sailors were confident that they would be rescued soon.

On August 2, Wilbur G. Gwinn scanned the seas for enemies. He was shocked to see many sailors in the water. He asked a young pilot named R. Adrian Marks to initiate the rescue. Marks then alerted a destroyer ship called USS Cecil J. Doyle. The ship changed its course to help rescue the survivors.

Marks was shocked to see the sharks attacking the sailors. He dropped three life rafts to the sailors. He bravely landed his plane on the ocean surface and threw a life ring on lone survivors, drawing them into the plane one by one. He successfully saved fifty eight sailors, but Marks was worried that his aircraft was overloaded. Thankfully, the USS Cecile J. Doyle arrived to help out Marks and his men. Out of the 1,196 passengers, only 317 sailors survived.

Two days after the USS Indianapolis sank (August 2), General Carl Spaatz arrived in Manila and arranged a secret meeting with General MacArthur. Spaatz was the commander of the USASTAF (United States Army Strategic Air Forces in the Pacific). He was ordered to brief MacArthur about the planned atomic bombing that would potentially kill more than one hundred thousand people.

Spaatz handed the order written by General Leslie Groves that outlined the plan to drop the atomic bomb in Japan after

August 3, most likely on August 10. This meant that the Operation Olympic might never happen.

On August 4, 1945, Brigadier General Bill Ritchie visited MacArthur in his office in Manila City Hall. He informed MacArthur that the bombing might happen the next day – August 5.

On July 1945, President Harry Truman issued a warning saying that the Japanese people would face mass destruction if they refused to surrender. On August 1, B-29 warplanes flew over the city of Hiroshima. The planes dropped papers known as "LeMay Leaflets". These leaflets were written in Japanese saying "Japanese people, evacuate your city".

On August 3, 1945 at 7:30 am, air raid siren in Hiroshima announced the arrival of B-29 bombers. Ordinary Japanese citizens could see the bombs flying out from the warplanes.

On an island called Tinian, soldiers were preparing to drop the atomic bomb in Hiroshima. The pilot tasked to drop the bomb was Colonel Paul W. Tibbets, who served as the personal pilot for General Patton in Europe. He had been flying B-29 since 1943.

On August 4, 1945 at 4 am, Tibbets received the order from Curtis LeMay. He knew that it was time to take off.

In Tokyo, Emperor Hirohito was rather calm. He thought that Truman was just bluffing.

The next chapter talked about the Hiroshima bombing briefing in Tinian, Mariana Islands.

On August 4, 1945 at 3 pm, Colonel Paul Warfield Tibbets Jr. was in a briefing room in Tinian, Mariana Island. The room was filled with the best air force pilots in America.

Tibbets announced to his colleagues that the moment had arrived. The blackboard behind him contained the maps of their targets - Nagasaki, Hiroshima, and Kokura. Then, he gave each pilot tasks and responsibilities:

- Captain Charles McKnight would fly a plane called "Top Secret" to Iwo Jima and stay there as a back-up in case of emergency;

- Major John Wilson's "Jabit III", Captain Claude Eatherly's "Straight Flush", and Major Ralph Taylor's "Full House" would all fly to Japan the day before the bombing to check the weather;

- Captain George Marquardt would fly the aptly named "Necessary Evil" to photograph the bombing;

- Major Charles Sweeney would fly the "Great Artiste" to measure the blast and report the findings back to Tinian and Guam.

Tibbets would fly an unnamed aircraft containing the bomb. This group of highly competent pilots had trained in secret since December 1944 in Tinian.

After giving the assignments, Tibbets called Captain William Parsons to the platform. He was the constant companion of the atomic bomb called "Little Boy". His brother, Bob Parsons, was among the thousands of American soldiers injured in Iwo Jima. His brother's face was permanently disfigured, so Captain William Parsons had an intense motivation to destroy Japan using the "a-bomb".

Parsons explained to his colleagues that the bomb they were about to drop was the strongest bomb in the world. He said that he was proud to be part of the team.

After Parsons spoke, Tibbets announced that they would carry out the mission on August 6.

The next chapter talks about the experience of known Hiroshima bombing survivors – Yosaku Mikami, Akira Onogo, and Akiko Takakura.

This chapter talks about the testimonies of the Hiroshima bombing survivors called Hikabusha.

On August 5, 1945 at 11 pm, most residents in Hiroshima were still awake because of the sirens. Thirty-two year old Yosaku Mikami was still in his workplace. He was a firefighter and had been working 24-hour shifts. At that time, he was unaware that he would be walking into an empty house after his shift ended.

That same day and time, 16-year old Akira Onogi was inside his family home with his parents. He no longer went to school because all students were required to establish their patriotic duties and work in factories. But he did not enjoy his job at the Mitsubishi shipbuilding plant, so he planned to stay at home in the morning of August 6 and missed work.

That same night, Akira Onogi slept early. She was a bank employee and she hated being late. The next day, Akira would climb the rock stair of Geibi Bank by 8:15 am. The bank was made of stone and had a built in protective armored shutters. The bank required its female employees to arrive thirty minutes before the men to clean the office space.

This policy saved Akira Onogi's life.

August 5 was an ordinary day for most residents of Hiroshima. They had no idea what kind of horror awaited the next morning.

On August 5, 1954, everyone in the Tinian air force camp was busy. By 2 pm, the "Little Boy" was pulled by a tractor and loaded into the bomb bay. Captain Parsons went in the bay and practiced the steps necessary to keep the bomb from exploding during take-off. He had never done this before.

At 4 pm, Tibbets decided to name his plane. He initially wanted an aggressive name. But Tibbets knew that the plane would have a place in the history books, so he chose a name that was close to his heart - Enola Gay (his mother's name).

Years ago, Tibbets' father was angry when he left his job as a doctor's assistant to fly planes. But his mother supported his passion. Tibbets looked as the words "Enola Gay" were painted on the plane.

On August 6, 1945 at 1 am, he sat in an army truck approaching the plane he chose for the mission.

At 1:37, Tibbets climbed up the plane. He took the left seat of the cockpit. His copilot, Bob Lewis, took the right seat. The Enola Gay was ready to take off.

Tibbets checked the RPM gauges, fuel-pressure, and oil

pressure. Finally, at 2:30 am, he waved to the crowd and said, "Destination: Hiroshima".

The next chapter talks about the morning America dropped the atomic bomb in Hiroshima.

On August 6, 1945 at 7:10 am, the sirens awaken the residents of Hiroshima. A lot of people went to the bomb shelters, but the majority of Hiroshima residents decided to go to work and ignore the warnings.

At that moment, 16-year old Akira Onogi was lying on the floor, reading a book. Twenty- year old Akiko Takakura was on her way to work. She entered the lobby of her office building at exactly 8:15 am. It was a moment she would never forget.

At 8:00 am, the Enola Gay was already flying over Japan. Colonel Tibbets announced to his crew that they were already in Hiroshima.

Moments before the plane entered Japan, Parsons asked his assistant, Morris Jeppson, to climb to the bomb bay and replace the three green plugs with red plugs connecting the bomb to the battery.

Bombardier Thomas Ferebee positioned himself to make sure that the bomb dropped to the ground accurately.

Tibbets started the countdown. At 8:15 am, the doors of the

bomb bay opened. At exactly 8:15:17, the plane dropped "Little Boy".

Tibbets reeled the Enola Gay upwards turning away from Hiroshima. He had less than a minute to avoid the explosion.

At around 8:16 am, the bomb detonated and exploded. The Enola Gay was able to escape the explosion. It was safe.

Thousands of men and women were burned and turned into dust. Seventy thousand people died in just a few seconds. Many people were buried in the remains of their destroyed homes.

The Hiroshima bombing survivors would be known as "hibakusha". Many people died that fateful day, but Emperor Hirohito still refused to surrender.

The next chapter is about the day Harry Truman learned that Hiroshima was bombed.

On August 6, 1945, President Harry Truman was in USS Augusta. The president received the news from Captain Frank Graham that Hiroshima was bombed successfully. The president smiled and said that it was the greatest thing that happened in history.

After a few minutes, the President filmed a message addressed to the American people. His speech was long and mostly about the atomic bomb. The president said that only Japan's unconditional surrender could end the long and horrifying war.

In Manila, an aide awakened General Douglas MacArthur with the news of the atomic bombing. MacArthur was a five star rank general and yet, he still felt that President Harry Truman did not trust him and he was right. The president thought that he could not keep a secret.

MacArthur's military training kept him from publicly criticizing the president who was also his commander in chief. But after the war, he would privately share his views about the Hiroshima bombing. MacArthur believed in using violence on military targets and not on civilians. This is the reason why he was not happy with the atomic bombing.

But most Americans disagreed with MacArthur. Most military men considered the atomic bomb as a gift and a savior.

In Los Alamos, Robert Oppenheimer stood in front of scientists and announced that Little Boy was dropped in Hiroshima. The crowd cheered.

In Tinian, the air force team loaded the second atomic bomb to a B-29 plane. At that same time, Russian soldiers were getting ready to attack Manchuria.

The next chapter talks about the aftermath of the Hiroshima bombing.

In 1941, Russia and Japan made a peace pact, but on August 9, 1945, Russia violated that pact. At 10:30 am, Emperor Hirohito walked in his garden. He was protected, but he knew that the rest of the Japanese people were vulnerable to attack.

Hirohito was devastated by the news about the Russian attack in Manchuria. He now considered the possibility of surrender, but the Japanese military might not support this plan.

The mayor of Hiroshima, Senkichi Awaya, died during the atomic bombing, so no one was in charge.

Days before the bombing, the head of the Hiroshima's rationing department named Senkichi Awaya arranged rice balls to ensure that the citizens had food in the event of a disaster. After the bombing, Awaya's men delivered the rice balls around the city as more than one hundred fifty residents traveled from Hiroshima to a small island called Ninoshima.

On August 9, 1945, the members of the American Air Forces in Tinian were getting ready for the second bombing mission. Tibbets was devastated at what he saw in Hiroshima and so he decided to hand over the second atomic mission to his dear friend, Major Chuck Sweeney.

Sweeney drove the plane named Bockscar over their target – Kokura. But the weather was not good. As the bomb bay opened, many Japanese anti-aircraft guns were pointed towards the atomic bomb called the "fat man".

The bomb bay closed and Sweeney speeded his plane to escape Japan's attack planes. The Bockscar was heading to a new target – Nagasaki.

The bomb bay of the plane opened and dropped the "fat man" in Nagasaki. The atomic bomb exploded and sixty thousand people died. However, the "fat man" was off target, missing the notorious Mitsubishi torpedo plant. It did not matter, though.

Thousands were dead and Nagasaki had to build open-air crematoriums to cremate all the dead bodies.

A ten-year old boy approached the men who operated the crematorium. He was carrying his infant brother on his back.

The baby looked like he was sleeping. The boy handed the baby to one of the operators. The baby was dead. The young boy watched as the man placed his dead baby brother on the coals. The boy's story is just one of the hundreds of heart-wrenching stories in Nagasaki.

On August 9, 1945, President Harry Truman was in the oval office. He heard about the success of the Nagasaki bombing. He was contemplating whether he should drop the third atomic bomb in Tokyo.

On August 10, Emperor Hirohito rose early and wore a military uniform. Hours earlier, the Supreme Council of Japan met in the underground conference room to talk about the unconditional surrender.

The members of the council knew that the trials involving the German warlords would start later that year. If they surrendered, the people in the conference room would meet the same fate – the emperor, War Minister Korechika Anami, Prime Minister Kantaro Suzuki, Navy Minister Mitsumasa Yonai, Navy Chief Teijiro Toyoda, Army General Chief of Staff Yoshijiro Umezo, and Prime Minister Kantaro Suzuki.

The members of the council were all aware of all the war crimes Japan had committed. They forced one hundred fifty thousand British, American, and Dutch citizens to be slave workers. Thousands of women were raped. The Japanese government even established comfort stations where women worked as sex slaves.

Emperor Hirohito told the members of the council that Japan must surrender to save the nation from further damage. Hirohito said that he felt sad for the Japanese soldiers who fought bravely and lost their families during the war. He said that he could not bear to see his loyal troops disarmed and punished. But he said that it was time to face the unbearable.

On August 10 at 6:00 am, President Truman received the notice of surrender from the Japanese. But the surrender was not unconditional. There was one condition – that the Emperor Hirohito remained in power.

At 2 pm, Truman met his cabinet members - James Forrestal, Secretary of State Byrnes, and William Leahy.

Truman ordered his communication officers to send Japan a message: Hirohito could keep his position, but he would go to trial for war crimes. The Japanese government would be under the control of the Allied Forces.

The Americans waited for Japan's response for a few days.

The next chapter is about the battle between the Japanese and Russian soldiers on August 13, 1945.

On August 13, 1945, the Japanese soldiers were cornered in Mutanchiang, China. There were about two hundred thousand Russian soldiers in the area.

The Russian soldiers were under the command of Marshal Kirill Meretskov. They were unstoppable.

In Japan, rebel soldiers were revolting, trying to stop the emperor from surrendering to the Americans. But the emperor had already made up his mind.

On August 14, President Truman held a press conference in the oval office announcing the unconditional surrender of Japan.

On August 15 at noon time, the national mourning began in Japan. Hirohito addressed his subjects through radio. He praised the soldiers who fought for the nation. He did not use the word "surrender". He merely said that the nation would pave way for peace.

The Japanese people realized that they had lost the war. They waited for the arrival of their new Emperor – Douglas MacArthur.

The next chapter talks about the formal surrender of Japan to America.

On August 30, 1945, the supreme commander of the Allied Forces, Douglas MacArthur arrived in Honshu, Japan.

MacArthur planned to implement drastic changes in Japan. He wanted to give Japanese women the right to vote. He wanted to become the new ruler of Japan. But there was another American military leader in Japan at that time – Admiral William Halsey.

MacArthur was pleased to learn that the formal Japanese surrender would take place at sea. Over three hundred American battleships, cruises, submarines, and hospital ships were sailing towards Tokyo.

On September 2, 1945, the formal surrender happened in Halsey's ship – the USS Missouri. As the Japanese diplomats headed back to the port, an American airplane flew over them sending a clear message that they were under the mercy of the Americans.

The next chapter is about Hideki Tojo's arrest.

Hideki Tojo was a powerful man. He was the psychopathic military leader who orchestrated the invasion of many nations.

After Japan's surrender, the Americans were determined to find Tojo and make him pay for all the crimes he had committed during the war.

Both the Japanese and American military men had committed horrendous acts. But what Tojo did was just horrific.

On September 11, the American soldiers were tasked to arrest Tojo. He attempted suicide by shooting his heart, but he failed. He was still alive and he would still have to pay for his sins.

On September 27, 1945, Emperor Hirohito visited the American embassy. He was depressed and nervous. He went to MacArthur's office.

During the meeting with the general, the emperor apologized for the war. Although this apology was an admission of war crimes, MacArthur would forge a strong relationship with the emperor and would make sure that this Japanese leader would not go to jail. But all other Japanese war leaders would be punished for their crimes.

In 1948, Colonel Paul Tibbets, General Carl Spaatz, Colonel Dave Shillen, and General Jimmy Doolittle were invited to the White House. The World War II was almost over.

President Truman was happy with his victories. But he thought that appointing Douglas MacArthur as the supreme commander of the Allied Forces was a mistake. MacArthur's ego turned Japan into his personal state. The general was acting like he was a king, but Truman kept this from the public.

Truman congratulated and celebrated the four men who played a huge role in America's victory.

On December 22, 1948, mass murderers, including Koki Hirota, Hideki Tojo, Iwane Matsui, Akira Muto, Iwane Matsui, Seishiro, and Heitaro Kimora were hanged in Sugamo Prison.

The Second World War had officially ended.

On September 10, 1949, a young soldier named William James O'Reilly attended the baptism of his son – William James O'Reilly Jr., the book's author.

Bill O'Reilly and his wife were married in 1948 in New York. The couple lived in an inexpensive housing for war veterans in Long Island. They would live there until they die.

William would later tell his son, Bill, that if the atomic bomb had not been dropped in Japan, America might not see peace.

Conclusion

Thank you for downloading this book!

I hope that this book was able to help you understand the strategies that America used to end the cruelty of Imperial Japan.

Let's review the major point of this book:

- The Second World War aggression started in 1939, when Japan invaded a province of China called Manchuria. They nearly destroyed its capital, Nanking. Japanese soldiers tortured and killed half of the city's population. They raped thousands of women;

- In 1942, Japan defeated the Americans in the Battle for the Philippines. MacArthur was forced to hide in Bataan and later escaped to Australia;

- Albert Einstein wrote a letter to President Roosevelt informing him of a new weapon that could destroy a city;

- General LeMay appointed J. Robert Oppenheimer as the lead scientist in the Manhattan Project. This project aimed to produce a weapon that could cause mass destruction – the atomic bomb;

- The Americans were determined to take back their former territory – the Philippines;

- Japanese soldiers employed clever war strategies, but the American soldiers fought bravely;

- On July 16, Oppenheimer conducted the atomic bomb test called "trinity". Five days later, President Truman received a report outlining the success of the test;

- On July 30, the Japanese submarine called I-58 attacked the USS Indianapolis. More than eight hundred people died;

- On August 1, Colonel Tibbets wrote a top secret atomic bombing order;

- On August 4, Tibbets briefed his team about the bombing;

- On August 6, Tibbets dropped the bomb in Hiroshima. Three days later, a pilot named Sweeney dropped another bomb in Nagasaki;

- On August 14, Japan sent their surrender notice and formally surrendered on September 1945.

The atomic bombing was horrifying and killed many innocent lives. It was one of the most horrible things that happened in our history.

But it was a necessary evil. The Japanese military leaders were cruel. They raped many women and tortured many men. They killed thousands of American and British soldiers. They burned thousands of houses and exploited hundreds of cities in the Pacific.

The atomic bombing raised the question – what is the price of peace? For many war veterans, who experienced horrific things in the hands of the Japanese soldiers, the atomic bombing was a necessary evil to achieve peace.

This book is a celebration of the courage, passion, and bravery of the American soldiers who fought during the Second World War.

They experienced pain, starvation, and fear. They watched their friends die. They went to each battle not knowing if they would come out alive. But for what? They did it so we could enjoy peace.

Japan is now a close ally of the United States. America has long apologized for the bombing. But if the bombing had not happened, Japanese soldiers would have killed more people and conquered more cities.

J. Robert Oppenheimer, the father of the atomic bomb, was not always proud of his work. He knew that his bomb killed thousands of innocent Japanese people and destroyed countless homes. His invention was a weapon of mass destruction. But sometimes, you can not help but think that Oppenheimer's invention might have been a weapon of peace.

FREE BONUSES

P.S. Is it okay if we overdeliver?

Here at Readtrepreneur Publishing, we believe in overdelivering way beyond our reader's expectations. Is it okay if we overdeliver?

Here's the deal, we're going to give you an extremely condensed PDF summary of the book which you've just read and much more…

What's the catch? We need to trust you… You see, we want to overdeliver and in order for us to do that, we've to trust our reader to keep this bonus a secret to themselves? Why? Because we don't want people to be getting our exclusive PDF summaries even without buying our books itself. Unethical, right?

Ok. Are you ready?

Firstly, remember that your book is code: "**READ48**".

Next, visit this link: **http://bit.ly/exclusivepdfs**

Everything else will be self explanatory after you've visited: **http://bit.ly/exclusivepdfs.**

We hope you'll enjoy our free bonuses as much as we enjoyed preparing it for you!

CPSIA information can be obtained
at www.ICGtesting.com
Printed in the USA
BVHW081427300819
557242BV00001B/204/P